which dog and how to keep it

essentials

charles cruft

foulsham
LONDON • NEW YORK • TORONTO • SYDNEY

foulsham

The Publishing House, Bennetts Close, Cippenham, Slough, Berkshire, SL1 5AP, England

ISBN 0-572-02775-3

Cover photograph by Ardea London/J. M. Labat

Illustrations of Bernese mountain dog, boxer, bull terrier, dobermann, Great Dane, Jack Russell, lhasa apso, rottweiler, saluki, shih tzu and Cardigan Welsh corgi by Michael Stringer.

All other illustrations from Duphar Kavak's dog chart. Decorative illustrations by Michael Stringer.

Printed in Great Britain by Creative Print and Design Wales, Ebbw Vale

Contents

Foreword

The name of Charles Cruft is legendary in the dog world, and he will always be remembered, of course, for the dog show that bears his name, which he started in 1891 and which is acknowledged to be the world's greatest dog show.

When Charles Cruft was writing about dog breeds and caring for dogs, he was way ahead of his time. He did not feel that a dog had to have a long pedigree to earn respect, but his respect for the animal included all members of any breed – or any combination of breeds. He also had a very practical attitude towards dogs and his writing presented good, solid facts about dogs and their care, based not only on his extensive theoretical knowledge but also on many years' experience. He was undoubtedly a true dog lover who wrote for people wanting to care properly for their dogs.

Now fully updated and extended to take account of modern knowledge and practice, this practical guide gives full information on how to choose the dog that will fit most comfortably into your family group, and how to give it the care, attention and training that will ensure that you and your pet enjoy a long and happy life together.

Chapter 1
Why Do You Want a Dog?

'Man's best friend is his dog.' The saying is as true today as it ever was: dogs make wonderful companions and friends. What's more, it has probably been true since the days of the Stone Age. We don't know exactly why our prehistoric ancestors first started to keep dogs, but it is likely to be for the same reasons that families keep them today: as a companion for the family and as a protector of the home. In time, dogs came to be trained as workers, and breeding became a business matter.

There are many reasons why you may be thinking about buying a dog, and there are very many different types and breeds to choose from. For this reason, it is worth spending a little time thinking about why you want a dog, and how you see its role in your life and that of your family. This will set the foundations for your eventual choice, as you will be able to match up the specific qualities of the individual breeds with your own needs and circumstances.

Many people say they are looking for a dog that will give them companionship. Certainly, in this role, a dog has no equal.

Through fair weather and foul, they remain the same: faithful at all times, sticking with you through thick and thin, and demanding very little in return beyond food, exercise and affection. Dogs of all kinds can provide this, from the toy dog nursed by its elderly owner, to the springer spaniel that accompanies its gamekeeper owner on his rounds.

Alternatively, you may want a dog for your child or children, in which case the dog is more often than not going to become an honorary member of the family. Children and dogs seem to have a common understanding that is quite beyond adult

comprehension and a puppy can be a great educational factor in a child's upbringing. It is important, however, that the child is not too young – it can be difficult to make very young children understand that they must not tease or hurt a dog.

Some people may also want a dog as a means of protection. The big breeds are often considered to be the best guard dogs, and certainly an intruder is more likely to be deterred by the appearance of a dog weighing upwards of 27 kg (60 lb), to say nothing of the bark that goes with it. Having said that, the little sealyham and dachshund can be very good watch dogs as far as sounding the alarm goes, and are very courageous, so either of these might be perfectly suited to your needs if you have a small house.

Finally, we must not leave out the subject of the show dog. There are people who do buy a dog for this purpose alone, although fortunately most combine this with the other reasons we have mentioned above. I say 'fortunately', because I think it is to a great extent a mistake to buy a dog solely to show. If appearance is made the primary motivation, then other good qualities are being rather pushed into the background – and a dog is no showman without these essential qualities of companionship, intelligence, playfulness and many others. In any event, the idea that there's a mint of money to be made from showing and breeding is generally without foundation. It is a wonderfully rewarding occupation for the committed, but certainly not an easy way to make a fortune.

Think carefully about why you want a dog – rather than, perhaps, a cat or another pet – as it is a big commitment and not one that you can easily reverse. You should be very sure about this first stage in the decision-making process. Consider what you expect of your dog and how you see its role in the family. Then you will be able to move on to the final selection of the breed of dog that is right for you.

Chapter 2
Choosing Your Dog

So you have decided that you really want a dog or a puppy to join your family. Now you have reached the practical stage where you must give the whole issue a great deal of serious thought and investigation. Remember: the average length of life of a dog is around 12 years and once you have taken one on there must be no question of a change of heart, unless it's for an absolutely unavoidable or unforeseen reason.

When it comes to choosing your dog, there are a number of factors that you need to consider. The sections of this chapter will cover them in turn. As you read through them, fill in your thoughts on the blueprint on pages 147–56 to help you narrow down your choice. Some of the questions are interrelated and so the answers you give will not always be a straightforward indication of suitability when taken individually. For example, if you have a relatively small house, this does not necessarily mean that you must have a small dog – you might still choose a slightly larger dog if you are able to give it plenty of exercise and its temperament is not too boisterous.

Read through each section and weigh up your situation from all points of view. This should give you a clearer idea of the sort of dogs that would be suitable for you. Then you can move on to the information on popular breeds on pages 33–145.

How much space do you have?

Broadly speaking, a small dog is suitable for a small house, whereas if you have a large house, you have the choice of a large or a small dog. However, even this first consideration is not totally inflexible. For example, if you have a moderately sized house but want a larger dog, you could compensate by choosing a very even-tempered and good-natured breed, but only if you are able – and prepared – to give it plenty of regular exercise. Under these circumstances, for example, a German shepherd dog can be less trouble than some of the small breeds, particularly as most of the big breeds are very docile animals. Even the biggest labrador will curl up in an incredibly small space – usually, it must be said, in front of the fire, keeping everyone else at a considerable distance. I must agree with my wife, however, that having a St Bernard in our cottage was beyond a joke, especially on wet days!

When you are thinking about this, do take into account the size of your garden; it may be small or large, or perhaps you have no garden at all. If the dog is to be allowed out in the garden, it must be secure so that the dog can run there in safety and not be able to escape through a hedge or broken fence. Bear in mind that really determined dogs of any size are able to jump high fences, creep under low wire and clamber over apparently insurmountable boundaries.

Do you like a tidy and clean house?

There's no reason at all why a dog should mean a dirty or untidy house, but if you like your house to be exceptionally spick and span, then you should rule out large, dominant and energetic dogs. Coming into an immaculate house with an Old English sheepdog after a walk through the park in the rain is unlikely to be your idea of a good combination! Also bear in mind that even the short-haired breeds shed some hair all the time, and of course, long-haired varieties will make that much more mess.

Of course, this does relate to how you train your dog from the start. If dogs are never allowed to sit on the sofa, then they will be quite happy with that and you'll never have to brush away dog hairs before your guests sit down! If they always come into the house through the utility room and stay there until they have been brushed down, that's what they will be used to and they won't hurtle into the beige-carpeted lounge. However, it's up to you to make sure you are consistent and start as you mean to go on.

How much time can you give to a dog?

You need to think about how a dog will fit into your daily routine. If you have a lot of available time – if you are retired, for example, or either you or your partner is at home all day – then you could consider a dog that demands a little more attention. If you are out at work all day, you must think about whether it is appropriate to have a dog at all. It may be that someone else can walk it during the day, but you will still have to consider how it will react to being on its own for considerable periods of time. You will certainly need to choose a placid breed that is happy to be left by itself, rather than a more lively type that may easily become bored and take its revenge on the furniture.

Do you go away a lot?

Spare a thought for holiday arrangements. Do you frequently go away for weekends or longer holidays? Will you be able to take a dog with you? If not, who will take care of the dog at those times? It can be very expensive to put a dog into kennels on a regular basis, and anyway, the dog may not necessarily enjoy being separated from you too often.

How active are you?

The larger and more active the dog, the more exercise it will need on a regular basis. If you go for a jog through the park every morning and could take the dog with you, then an active breed will readily fit into your lifestyle. On the other hand, if you do not take regular exercise – but perhaps want the dog to encourage you to take a daily walk – you need to think about where and when your outings will fit into your routine. If you are elderly or unable to take long walks, then obviously you must think about a smaller canine companion. Whatever the size of your dog, you will both benefit from regular exercise, and it may be just the encouragement you need to promote your own healthy lifestyle!

Think about whether you will expect the children to take the dog for regular walks, in which case you might want to choose a slightly smaller breed, and certainly to ensure that it can be well trained so that it can be kept under control at all times.

Don't forget that the dog will need to be exercised regardless of anything else that is going on. It makes no difference to the dog that it is dark in the mornings, that it is pouring with rain, or that you are late home from work and it's your birthday. Having a dog is a big commitment – but if you are prepared to make that commitment, it's a very rewarding one.

Can you train it?

All dogs need training – there is no way round this one – and it is a time-consuming and occasionally very frustrating process. If you decide to train the dog yourself, you will need plenty of time and patience. The alternative is to take it to classes, which is a good idea if you do not have much experience with dogs, but is not an easy way out: you will be expected to learn alongside your dog and put in lots of practice between classes.

Whatever method you choose, you must be prepared to put in quite a lot of work or you will end up with a badly behaved and probably very unhappy pet. You, and everyone in the family, must be firm and consistent from the start. Don't play rough-and-tumble games in the lounge with a puppy, or it will want to play tug-of-war with the best cushions when it grows up. If you allow it into the bedroom because it cries when you shut it in the kitchen at night, it will take that as its right and you will have a very hard time breaking the habit.

If you know that you are a soft touch, and you still want a dog, it is particularly important that you steel yourself to set the rules early on. To make thing easier for all concerned, choose a dog that is relatively easy to train and does not require very firm handling, otherwise everyone will soon work out who's boss – and it won't be you!

What about the children in your family?

The make-up of your family is also important in your choice, and you should think about how they are all going to be involved in caring for your pet. Are you going to share the walks, the feeding and the grooming? Or will it all fall to you? Are you going to have some sort of rota so that everyone takes their turn? Are your children old enough and responsible enough to take the dog out on their own? What will happen if the children have a coursework assignment to finish and don't have time to take their turn exercising the dog?

If you have very young children, do think about whether it would be worth waiting a year or so before buying a dog. Very young children – with the fondest of intentions – do not understand how to deal with animals, and a friendly pat on the head, slightly misdirected, can become a poke in the eye, which will make the most placid dog turn on the child. Once they are a little older, a child and a dog make the most wonderful of companions. In any event, if you have young children, you must take care to select a mild-tempered breed.

Does anyone in the family suffer from an allergy or illness that could be affected by a dog? Perhaps this might mean you should have a short-haired rather than a long-haired breed, or, better still, one of the woolly-coated breeds, such as a poodle.

Where will the dog fit in the family structure?

Dogs are pack animals and will find their niche in the family structure, often favouring one member. This is especially true of particular breeds. Think about which member of the family is likely to take most care of the dog, and what kind of dog they will relate to. For example, if your teenage daughter is likely to be the regular dog-walker, a large, strong dog with an assertive temperament may not be the best choice.

Do you have other pets?

If there are other pets already in the family, especially other dogs, then the needs of all the animals must be considered. The new dog will have to establish its place in the hierarchy of pets, just as it does with the family. So, for example, it's not a good idea to buy a male dog that will want to be in a dominant position if you already have another male dog, as they could be territorial in their instinctive need to be 'top dog'.

Puppies and kittens tend to get on well together from the start, but an adult dog may not react well to a cat in the house – or vice versa! Smaller animals – gerbils or hamsters, for example – need to be kept safely out of the dog's way.

There's more information on how to introduce your new dog to other pets on pages 186–7.

What is your budget?

There are two elements to this: the initial cost of buying the dog, and the cost of looking after it. Once you have narrowed down your choice of breed, find out what you should be expected to pay for that breed – the prices will vary enormously. Call the local animal shelter and research the costs of adult dogs or puppies if you are buying from that source. If you are looking for a dog to show or breed, then obviously you are considering a much higher initial outlay, and should speak with specialist breeders and look into the subject of cost in more detail.

Think through the basic costs of maintaining a dog, and talk to friends about how much it will cost on a day-to-day basis. Simply put, the larger the dog, the bigger the food bills. You will also need to consider basic equipment (see pages 164–70), routine veterinary bills and kennel charges for holidays. You may also want to consider a pet insurance policy (see page 200).

Do you want a puppy or a dog?

For many people, buying a puppy is the best choice, as you can train the dog yourself and get it used to your own particular circumstances at the earliest possible age. There's also the fun element of enjoying the playful nature and delightful looks of a young animal. You can watch and guide the progress of its development, a fascinating study in itself. If you are buying a dog to show or breed, you will almost certainly want to buy it as a puppy. However, you must take the responsibility for caring for the puppy as it grows up, and for training it to become a well-behaved and happy adult dog. Puppies – by their very nature – are boisterous, lively and time-consuming.

Note that many different breeds look very much alike when they are anything up to eight weeks old, so it is important that you are not misled by this when making your choice. If you are buying a pedigree dog, then you will know the breed, the sire and dam, and can make a fairly accurate assessment of the adult size of the dog. However, if you are buying a cross-breed, then you must be very careful not to buy what you believe will be a small dog but which, in fact, turns out to be a gun dog, or something even larger. Don't buy a puppy solely on its attractive looks; remember that, like a child, it won't stay that way for long. It will soon be an adult dog who will be living for years in your household, and few real dog lovers would have the heart to turn out a much bigger dog than they bargained for, having raised the animal for a year from that attractive puppy stage.

If you decide to buy an adult dog, on the other hand, you must remember that many of its habits and behavioural tendencies will already have been established, so there are different questions that need to be answered. For example, has it been ill-treated? Is it house-trained? (Don't assume because it's adult that it is.) Try to get as much information as possible about its background and history before you make your decision to buy it.

Should you buy a dog or a bitch?

In the natural hierarchy of the dog world, male dogs tend to be more territorial and may not tolerate other dogs. They may also be more determind. On the other hand, a bitch will tend to be more submissive and two bitches can live happily together (although fights between bitches can be more serious). Think about this aspect when you are considering the temperament of the animal you choose for your family. Male dogs also tend to be larger and therefore stronger, take up more space and need more food, so you might think about this when working out your budget!

Should you buy more than one dog?

Sex is also important in relation to buying more than one dog, and buying two dogs – as opposed to a dog and a bitch or two bitches – should be very carefully considered and discussed, as it could be a recipe for a unhappy family. Two dogs are likely to compete for superiority in the family group, and this can encourage them to show their more aggressive tendencies. Alternatively, it may simply result in an uneasy truce, rather than the comfortable relationship you had hoped for.

Do you want a pedigree or a cross-breed?

If you are considering showing or breeding, then obviously you will choose a pedigree dog. If so, you will obviously be familiarising yourself with the qualities of the breed – both physically and temperamentally – while you are making your choice of dog.

In the UK, The Kennel Club is the governing body that sets the standards for all breeds of dog, organises shows and maintains a register of pure-bred dogs. When a breeder hands over a pedigree, it does not necessarily mean that your dog has been registered with The Kennel Club, although most breeders do register their litters before selling them. Obtaining The Kennel Club registration document for your dog will authenticate its pedigree. If you are in any doubt about anything relating to a pedigree or a breeder, you can always consult The Kennel Club for confirmation. Full pedigrees go back several generations.

Many people, however, choose a cross-breed and these can and do offer their owners just as much in companionship, and, for that matter, intelligence too. The downside is that you do not have an established pattern of characteristics to help you when making your choice of a puppy. Ideally, you should know

BREED Boxer

SEX Dog

COLOUR & MARKINGS Red/One/White

DATE OF BIRTH: 24/10/93

BREEDER Mr + Mrs Rogers

KENNEL CLUB No. TS464208T04

DATE OF REGISTRATION 26/11/93.

KENNEL CLUB STUD No. _____

OWNER _____

ADDRESS _____

PARENTS	GRANDPARENTS	GREAT GRANDPARENTS	GT. GT. GRANDPARENTS
SIRE Jonathan Hops Lott K.C. no: S1804609502	**Sire** Buckskin Boy the Girl at Glaphill	**Sire** Glaydon Klashill the Gladiator	**Sire** Glaydon Kudra Beech Boy of Allendel **Dam** of Garrett Qudor
		Dam Buckskeps no-no Nantie	**Sire** Buckskin Qualie **Dam** Buckska Rupert
	Dam Jonathan Grace Justine	**Sire** Glaydon Klapark Glorious Grame	**Sire** Glaydon Breeth flint **Dam** Gregory's old
		Dam Gruidatari of Larashay	**Sire** Kaldanaye **Dam** Butterfly Ros.s
DAM Aozis Affinity K.C. no: R4551064	**Sire** Red trade of Hawaii	**Sire** Red Devil at Hawaii	**Sire** Wesilince of Candicotti **Dam** Puncatt Carried
		Dam Hawaii	**Sire** Sunshine **Dam** Maryon Glendan Laris Jale
	Dam Krisky Dove Aozis	**Sire** Kuban Jaunt Prince	**Sire** Renton flire **Dam** De trys Supreme **Sire** Butterfly Lucky **Dam** Sheila
		Dam Crisky Dove Aozis	**Sire** Larashay's Haze **Dam** Cleopatra of Aozis

Printed by Dog Breeders Associates

I certify this Pedigree to be correct to the best of my knowledge.

Signed _____ R.J. Rogers   Date _____ 18/12/93.

both the parents so you have some idea of what the puppy is going to grow into. For example, if you are intent on having a small dog, it's no good buying the offspring of a small mother if you don't know anything about the father of the litter. He may have been enormous and your small puppy could grow to be twice the size of its mother.

What are the characteristics of the breed?

Whether you decide to buy a pedigree or a cross-breed, you should find out as much as you can about both the physical and temperamental characteristics of the dog before you make your choice. You will find all the information you need on many popular breeds on pages 33–156. You can also look up information on the web, talk to breeders and animal carers, and talk to other people you know who have dogs.

Dogs come in all kinds of sizes and shapes and with all kinds of personalities, and it is essential to match your needs with those of the breed that's right for you. A labrador is a wonderful, easy-going companion for an active family. But despite its gentle nature, it has huge energy and would be a liability in a small house with a quiet, elderly owner who prefers a gentle stroll round the park to a run through the woods.

These are the main areas you need to consider:

Size: Think about the predicted adult size of the dog or bitch.

Gender: Consider the temperamental and size differences between a dog and a bitch.

Energy levels: Some dogs are high-energy and need space to run and regular, vigorous exercise; others are quieter and generally more contented.

Coat: The longer the coat, the more grooming the dog will require. It may also need regular clipping.

Intelligence: This will affect how easy the dog is to train as well as its general temperament.

Sociability: Some dogs are better than others in a family environment and react more favourably to children.

Type: The Kennel Club group to which the dog belongs (see pages 34–6) gives an indication of the jobs for which the dogs were originally bred, and can be useful in offering guidance on their likely character.

Don't just think about these elements in isolation. Relate them to what you have discovered about your own needs as a family while reading the earlier sections. For example, a longer coat will mean more of your time spent grooming, and more money spent on professional grooming or clipping; you'll have to take an energetic dog on longer and more regular walks where there's plenty of space for it to run.

Inherited diseases

It is almost inevitable that congenital defects will occur in some animals. The passing on of genetic or congenital problems is to some extent the breeder's responsibility, but may not be their fault, especially if this is the first time the defect has occurred in their strain of dogs. It makes good sense, therefore, to have your newly purchased puppy checked by a vet.

Some problems, such as weak knee joints, badly aligned jaws and undescended testes, may not have been noticeable to you but may cause suffering and expense later. Your vet will be able to tell you whether any condition is likely to cause immediate or long-term problems and what may be done to correct it. If it is serious, he may advise you to contact the breeder or even to return the puppy.

There are particular problems that are common in certain breeds, and the breeder should be aware of these and will do as much as possible to breed away from them.

Hip dysplasia

This is a condition of deformed hip joints that can lead to lameness and chronic pain. It is particularly prevalent in German shepherd dogs, retrievers, great Danes, Old English sheepdogs, Pyrenean mountain dogs, rottweilers and collies, although other large breeds may also be affected. If you are considering buying any of these breeds, you should ask your vet to check its hips.

The British Veterinary Association has a special hip-scoring system based on X-rays evaluating each dog's hips. A breeder should be able to provide you with a BVA hip score for both the sire and dam of your puppy. This will certainly be necessary if you are thinking of breeding from it at a later date.

Eye conditions

There are a number of serious inherited eye conditions, some of which may lead to painful blindness. Collies and Shetland sheepdogs are susceptible to collie eye anomaly and can be screened at eight weeks, if you are thinking of breeding. Other eye diseases affect cocker spaniels, basset hounds, bloodhounds, Cavalier King Charles spaniels, English springer spaniels, retrievers, labradors and poodles.

Ear conditions

Some white-coated dogs may be deaf in one or both ears. This is a serious handicap and such dogs need very special care. Puppies may be tested for hearing at eight weeks of age. Breeds most affected are dalmations, white boxers and bull terriers.

Other conditions

Particular breeds may also be affected by other conditions, such as skin problems in West Highland terriers, heart problems in Cavalier King Charles spaniels and boxers, and ear problems in large spaniels. Some breed clubs operate their own screening schemes.

Always ask both the breeder and your vet about breed-related diseases before you make your choice of puppy.

How do you judge the characteristics of a cross-breed?

If you are thinking about a cross-breed puppy, you can still use the breed information to help you make your choice. You may know the breeds of both the sire and dam, in which case you have a good basis for assessing the likely physical and temperamental characteristics of the puppy. Remember, though, that the puppies could bear a stronger resemblance to one or other of their parents – as in *Lady and the Tramp* – rather than being a neat mixture of the two.

Even if you don't know the puppy's sire, you should know its dam and be able to assess her physical and temperamental characteristics by talking to the owner, and relating them to the closest breed information you can.

If you are choosing an adult dog, the physical characteristics will be there in front of you to assess, but you should take care to discuss the temperament of the dog with the person who has been caring for it. Try to find out as much as you can about its background and how it has reacted to any changes in its life. The staff at reputable pet shelters are expert at assessing dogs and will not offer you an animal that they do not believe is suitable for you. Their primary interest is in finding the best possible home for the dog, so they will want to make sure you match up to the dog's blueprint for a perfect owner!

Making a good choice

Here's an example of how you can successfully put all these elements together in order to make a good choice.

Peter and Jenny Smith and their two children, aged seven and five, live in a pleasant, suburban semi-detached house with a medium-sized garden. The children are at school and Jenny works part-time at the local school. Peter works in the nearby town and does not travel with his job, so is home at a reasonable time in the evenings. They enjoy country walks and take family holidays in their caravan.

The children have been pestering their parents for quite some time for a puppy of their own, and the parents have now decided that the children are old enough for them to give the issue serious consideration. They have already laid down some ground rules. Firstly, they have decided that the puppy should not be a Christmas present since everyone will be busy with the Christmas celebrations, there will be lots of visitors and outings and consequently not much time for a puppy. Secondly, they have insisted that the choice of dog is up to the parents, as the children are not old enough to think through all the implications of the choice and will probably choose on looks alone. Peter is slightly worried about the garden and what it is going to look like after a dog has been running round in it for six months, and Jenny knows she will have to expect more housework on wet days.

So what are they looking for?

Size: A relatively small dog will fit in with their home and be less of a problem in the garden.

Gender: A bitch will tend to be more submissive and could be easier for the children to control.

Energy levels: These should be moderate rather than high to fit with their lifestyle and the ages of the children.

Coat: To minimise grooming and mess on wet days, a short-coated breed would be best.

Intelligence: The dog does not need any special skills, but a general level of intelligence is necessary so that it can be trained to be well behaved.

Sociability: A high level of sociability is an essential quality for any family dog.

Type: Probably a dog from the pastoral group (see page 35) would be most suitable.

There are at least a dozen breeds they could choose from, but the Smiths choose a Welsh corgi. It is a fairly small dog with a short, trouble-free coat, is clean in its habits, does not require long walks, and has a reasonable appetite. It is a very sharp and sociable little house dog.

Getting more information

Read all about the popular breeds on pages 33–145 and look in other books and on the web. Visit dog shows, talk to breeders and talk to other people who own dogs. If you are buying a pedigree, study the detailed standards laid down by The Kennel

Club for the particular breeds you are interested in. If you have friends with dogs, spend the day with them, or invite them to bring their dog to your home for a day or a weekend. In this way you can actually experience the practicalities of dog-ownership, for example, getting up on a cold, dark, wet winter's morning to take it for its early walk.

Making the final choice

Once you have narrowed down your selection and you are confronted with a litter of puppies, it becomes even harder to choose, as you look at their lovely little faces and have to select or reject them! The breeder will certainly help you. They will already have found out as much as they can about you and the sort of home you have, so may well make your life easy by making the match for you. Trust their experience as they will have come to know the puppies well during their first few weeks and will have a great deal of experience in matching puppies to families.

All puppies should look healthy and active, with bright eyes and a wet nose. They should move well and have a good coat. They should have been checked by a vet and have been given a clean bill of health.

Try to interact with the puppies so that you can judge their character by their behaviour. Concentrate on one puppy at a time and don't rush your decision. See how it reacts to the following stimuli.

- Clap your hands to encourage the puppy to come to you.
- Crouch down and gently stroke the puppy's back.
- Roll the puppy on its back and hold it there for a few seconds.
- Stand up and walk away from the puppy, making sure it sees you walk away.
- Make a sharp sound.
- Roll a ball in front of the puppy.
- Shake a piece of fabric or string in front of the puppy.

At one extreme, an aggressive puppy will tend to bite and may be quite noisy. It will be very quick to react to anything, but is likely to snap and bark. These puppies make good working dogs but need experienced and firm handling and are not really the best choice for a family.

Most families will be looking for a puppy that reacts quickly and is interested in what you are doing, but it should be confident rather than aggressive, more likely to lick your hand than bite you. It should quickly catch on to what you expect; when you throw the ball, for example, it should bring it back – although it is unlikely to give it to you.

If any animal seems friendly and reacts well but is a little nervous and more submissive in its behaviour, it may be more suitable for an owner who can offer a quieter lifestyle with plenty of regular companionship and affection to encourage it to grow in confidence. This may be the puppy for an elderly person, for example.

At the other end of the extreme, an animal that wanders away and does not appear to be interested in what you are doing is likely to be very independent. This is not an animal that needs much companionship, nor is it likely to be overly responsive to affection. These will probably not be good family pets, but are better placed where they have a job to perform that does not depend so much on human contact.

Chapter 3
Popular Breeds

This chapter will give you more detailed information on many of the most popular dog breeds in order to help you make the right choice for your family. The Kennel Club in the UK recognises specific breeds and sets detailed standards for each breed, so if you are thinking of buying a dog for showing or breeding, you need to refer to those precise standards in order to ensure that you find a good specimen. They are all available on their web site: www.the-kennel-club.org.uk

If you are buying a dog simply as a family pet, the finer points may not be so important. However, whether as a pet or for showing, intelligence and temperament are just as important as looks, and you must ensure that the animal you choose is the right one for you.

For each breed, the silhouette gives you an idea of the size of the dog in relation to an adult. We have also given approximate heights and weights for the dogs. Where there is a Kennel Club standard, this has been quoted; otherwise, a representative range of height and weight has been given. In general, bitches are smaller and lighter than dogs.

Breed types

All dogs are divided by The Kennel Club into seven main groups: gun dogs, hounds, pastoral, terriers, toy, utility and working. In addition, there are some breeds that are popular but are not registered with The Kennel Club, such as the Jack Russell.

Gun dogs

Cocker spaniel, field spaniel, pointer, German short-haired pointer, English setter, Gordon setter, Irish setter, golden retriever, labrador retriever, English springer spaniel, Irish water spaniel, weimaraner.

These dogs were bred to help men when they were out shooting: their tasks were scenting and flushing out the game, and retrieving it. Sizes and coats vary tremendously, but they tend to be in the middle size and always have a soft mouth. They are intelligent, reliable and take well to training, but they tend to be active dogs.

Hounds

Afghan hound, basset hound, beagle, bloodhound, borzoi, deerhound, smooth- and long-haired dachshund, elkhound, foxhound, greyhound, Irish wolfhound, saluki, whippet.

These hunting dogs were bred to use scent and to work in a pack. From the very large bloodhounds to small dachshunds, they tend to be intelligent and active.

Pastoral

Border collie, rough and smooth collie, German shepherd dog, Old English sheepdog, Pyrenean mountain dog, samoyed, Shetland sheepdog, Welsh corgi.

This new grouping used to be listed with the working dogs, but are now a division on their own, including dogs that traditionally worked on pastoral land. Colour, coat and size all vary considerably, but they are very active dogs that prefer to lead a busy life and need plenty to keep them active and amused.

Terriers

Airedale terrier, Bedlington terrier, border terrier, bull terrier, cairn terrier, Dandie Dinmont terrier, wire and smooth fox terrier, Irish terrier, Kerry blue terrier, Manchester terrier, Scottish terrier, sealyham, Skye terrier, Welsh terrier, West Highland white terrier.

Originally bred to hunt vermin, these are active dogs, usually small to medium-sized with a wide variety of coat styles. Full of confidence and quite feisty, they can be aggressive if not well trained and controlled. Some of them love to dig.

Toy

Chihuahua, King Charles spaniel, papillon, miniature pinscher, pekinese, pomeranian, pug, Yorkshire terrier.

Bred as miniature companions for ladies and high-born families, these are now popular with many people. All are tiny dogs, many – but not all – have longer coats, and they often have a spirit out of all proportion to their diminutive size.

Utility

Boston terrier, bulldog, chow-chow, dalmatian, keeshond, lhasa apso, poodle, schnauzer, shih tzu.

This classification is very diverse – almost used if the dog does not fit anywhere else – so there is a great deal of variety in all aspects of the dogs' looks and characters. They tend to be in the middle range of size.

Working

Bernese mountain dog, boxer, dobermann, Great Dane, mastiff, rottweiler, Saint Bernard.

Intelligent and ideal for training, these dogs are used to having a job to do and expending a great deal of energy in carrying it out. They are tremendously loyal but need firm handling and plenty to keep them occupied.

Afghan hound

Height to shoulder: 63–74 cm (25–29 in)
Weight: 27–32 kg (60–70 lb)
Group: Hound

Glamour in the dog world comes in many forms, but the Afghan must be in the top ten of anybody's list. Originally used as a hunting dog by the hill tribesmen of Afghanistan, it is quite unique in appearance. The long silky coat extends to the feet, so the legs have a 'baggy' appearance when covered with an abundance of hair. The ears are well feathered and pendulous, the face is narrow and smooth, and the tail is well carried and curving at the tip. The breed is very graceful in movement and apart from its long coat it very much resembles a greyhound with its long head and dark eyes. Afghans are all colours, most commonly gold.

Highly intelligent, the Afghan is also fairly highly strung and difficult to train, and tends to be aloof. It is a large dog and needs a lot of exercise, so you need both the time and surroundings to take the dog for long and frequent runs. With such a long coat, it obviously requires a lot of regular grooming.

Airedale terrier

Height to shoulder: 56–61 cm (22–24 in)
Weight: 18–23 kg (40–51 lb)
Group: Terrier

The present Airedale terrier originated in the valley of the River Aire in Yorkshire, England, and is the result of a cross between a native hound and a terrier. The breed is quite a powerful one and is the largest of the terriers. The dog has every characteristic of a smaller terrier with a hard, wiry coat, black and tan in colour, which needs regular stripping as it is a double coat. The coat is waterproof and sheds twice a year. The Airedale has small V-shaped ears, a square muzzle, a short and straight back and perfectly straight legs. It is a big-boned dog and stands strong and firm. It has small eyes, a thickset neck, a flat skull and long head with a deep and powerful jaw. The tail is usually docked to about half its length.

The Airedale is a natural guard dog, intelligent, alert, quick of movement and fearless but not aggressive. The police forces have used these dogs with success. They are very muscular and active, so need a lot of exercise, but make great companions and good family dogs for those with plenty of energy.

Basset hound

Height to shoulder: 33–38 cm (13–15 in)
Weight: 20–32 kg (44–70 lb)
Group: Hound

This is very much a dog of character, and is in a class of its own. It has a long and powerful body with great depth through the ribs, the neck is thick-set and strong. The head gives an appearance of being almost dome-shaped, which is probably accentuated by the long, narrow snout; the brow and sides of the cheeks are very wrinkled, the long ears are set low and should hang very evenly in folds; the eyes are deep set. The short front legs fit closely, inclining inwards from the elbow to the knee, and outwards from there to the feet, which are large and also turned outward. For a small dog, the basset is quite muscular, and strong. The coat colour is hound marked (meaning it has a white background, with broken markings of shades of brown), black, tan and white or lemon and white. The coat is flat and smooth, and has a fine, 'polished' appearance.

Known as an affectionate and placid breed, the basset can in fact be very stubborn at times, so needs thorough training and a firm owner. They are strong dogs so perhaps are less suited to a family with young children. Although they are likely to get very muddy because of their short stature, their short coat is easy to groom.

Beagle

Height to shoulder: 33–41 cm (13–16 in)
Weight: 8–14 kg (18–31 lb)
Group: Hound

These dogs have always enjoyed great popularity, both working in the country and on the show bench, but they are now becoming more popular as pets. The beagle is a very old breed indeed and has been recognised for some centuries. Although very much a hound in appearance, these smaller dogs in no way resemble the foxhound. The head is powerful and dome-shaped, with long ears. The beagle has fine, short hair, a deep chest and rather short body; the ribcage is deep and strong and the dog is very muscular. The forelegs are straight, and the feet round and well padded for cross-country work. Colouring is

'hound marked' in a variety of typical brown and white markings and the coat is short, dense and waterproof.

The beagle is an intelligent, even-tempered and sociable dog, so makes a good companion. However, it needs someone who can handle it firmly, as it is also determined and confident. Very strong and active, with an abundance of stamina, it needs plenty of regular exercise as boredom may lead to destructive behaviour and wandering. The short coat is quite easy to groom and does not require any special treatment.

Bedlington terrier

Height to shoulder: About 41 cm (16 in)
Weight: 8–10 kg (18–22 lb)
Group: Terrier

Another less well-known breed, the build of the Bedlington is similar to the whippet, but the coat is more like that of its cousin, the Dandie Dinmont. The head and arched body are probably the most distinctive features, and it is often said to look like a lamb. The muzzle is long and tapering and the head narrow, with almost a straight line from the top of the skull to the tip of the nose. The body is moderate in length with a flat, deep ribcage. The ears are medium sized and lie flat on the cheeks. It has a silky topknot, not unlike the Dandie's. The coat is very distinctive, thick and firm (the official term is 'linty') but not wiry, standing well out from the skin. Usual colours are blue (dark grey), liver (dark brown) or sandy, with or without tan. Those with a darker coat have dark eyes, those with a lighter coat tend to have lighter, more hazel eyes.

The Bedlington is an intelligent, affectionate and good-tempered dog with lots of confidence, so it can make a good family dog. Its medium size means it is not too demanding of exercise, but it should be regularly groomed and clipped.

Bernese mountain dog

Height to shoulder: 58–69 cm (23–27 in)
Weight: 40–44 kg (88–97 lb)
Group: Working

The Bernese mountain dog was originally used as a cattle herd by Swiss farming communities. The farmers also used the dogs to pull their farm carts to market. It is quite a large dog, strongly built, with a long, wavy coat, which is black with tan and white markings. The head is strong with a flat skull and the eyes are dark. It has a bushy tail, carried high.

Bernese mountain dogs are usually hard working and active. They are even-tempered, self-confident, good-natured and friendly. Never aggressive, they are perfect gentlemen, kind and courteous but, being large dogs, they do need a lot of space. Not a noisy dog, the Bernese makes a perfect companion and devoted family pet.

Bloodhound

Height to shoulder: 58–69 cm (23–27 in)
Weight: 36–50 kg (80–110 lb)
Group: Hound

This breed is said to have been introduced into Britain during the Norman conquest. Certainly, we know these dogs come from France, where they were bred as sporting dogs, using the ability to follow scent for which they are so famous. The bloodhound is one of the oldest of sporting breeds. Their most conspicuous feature is the great looseness of skin, particularly around the head and jowl. The ears are long and silky and set low. The eyes give the appearance of being bloodshot, but this is

in fact due to the down-drag of its lips (known as flews), which causes the inner skin of the lower lid to be shown. The back is long and strong. The dog has heavy bones and straight legs.

A big dog, the bloodhound's rightful place is the country, where it is happiest. They have been used with great success for tracking, and consequently are employed by the police – a well-trained dog can use a scent up to 24 hours old. Noble and dignified, they generally have an even temperament and affectionate nature but can be a little sensitive and reserved so would not necessarily make a good family pet.

Border collie
Height to shoulder: 51–53 cm (20–21 in)
Weight: 14–22 kg (31–48 lb)
Group: Pastoral

This working dog has been known for hundreds of years, but it got its name in the late nineteenth century when it was one of the most successful breeds in the early sheepdog trials in the England/Scotland border counties. As with many working dogs, border collies were bred to produce good animals for the job of herding sheep, but were recognised by The Kennel Club to be included on the breed register in 1976. An attractive dog, usually black and white, with a long, glossy coat with short hair on the face and legs, it has a dense topcoat and a soft, weather-resistant undercoat. The head is broader and shorter than that of the rough or smooth collies. Strong and graceful, the border collie is an active dog with plenty of stamina. It is internationally known as one of the best sheepdog breeds and has been used as part of the breeding stock for the Australian kelpie and the Australian cattle dog.

The border collie is a tenacious and energetic working dog, needing an enormous amount of exercise and stimulation. It thrives on company and will participate in any activity. Devoted to its master, it is the type of dog that needs to work to be happy and will never be content to sit at home all day. It is very much a working dog rather than a family pet.

Border terrier
Height to shoulder: 25–28 cm (10–11 in)
Weight: 6–7 kg (13–15½ lb)
Group: Terrier

This great little sporting breed is one of the top 20 breeds registered with The Kennel Club. As indicated by its name, it hails from the Northumberland/Scotland border and is a great and established favourite there, where it is bred for earthing

foxes and other creatures, and will tackle anything in the vermin world. The head resembles that of an otter, its breadth being accentuated by a short muzzle. It usually has a short, hard, corn-coloured or black and tan coat. It can run happily alongside a horse and cover long distances each day.

Overall, this is a popular terrier that fits very well into the average home, although it is probably happiest in the country. It is great on a farm or similar property where the owner needs to keep rats under control. It has a loyal and courageous temperament, but it is also very active and enthusiastic so needs firm handling if it is not to become noisy and destructive.

Borzoi

Height to shoulder: 69–74 cm (27–29 in)
Weight: About 48 kg (105 lb)
Group: Hound

The borzoi comes from Russia where it was popular in the court of the Tsars and kept in packs by the nobility for hunting wolves. It remains popular in its native land, and in many others now as well, although it is more common as a show breed than as a pet. Borzois are handsome-looking animals and are among the biggest of breeds. They have the lines of a greyhound in almost every respect and are conspicuous for their attractive coat and colouring. They are very fast, as they were bred to run with horses, with a strong build. Their coat is silky and inclined to curl; white, fawn and white, and lemon and white are the most common colours. The head is very long and sleek, and really artistic in shape, with small ears placed well back. The chest is narrow and very deep, the back well arched with very strong loins and straight front legs. It is built for speed and stamina rather than weight, so tends to be fairly bony, and it has perfect balance. Without doubt, this is one of the most aristocratic of breeds.

Sensitive and alert, the borzoi's gentle nature and intelligence make it a good companion, although it can tend to be aloof. It is a large dog and needs a lot of exercise to keep it healthy and happy and the long coat requires a lot of careful grooming, especially in male dogs, as their coat is longer. All in all, this is more of a show dog than one for the average family.

Boston terrier

Height to shoulder: 38–43 cm (15–17 in)
Weight: 6.5–11 kg (14–24 lb)
Group: Utility

This American breed was first recognised over a century ago, and remains more popular in the USA than elsewhere, being one of America's most famous breeds. As can be guessed from its appearance, the original cross was an English bull terrier with a bulldog, and the results are a fairly even distribution of both sets of features, and are also similar to the French bulldog. A very compact little dog, with a short head and short, low tail, it has a short, smooth coat in brindle and white or black and white. The weight varies considerably, so much so that the official standard divides the breed into three weight categories.

Easy to maintain, the Boston terrier makes an alert and happy house dog with a highly developed intelligence. However, it can be determined and strong-willed, and its adventurous nature may lead it to wander, so firm training is essential. Its small to medium size means it needs a moderate but not excessive amount of exercise.

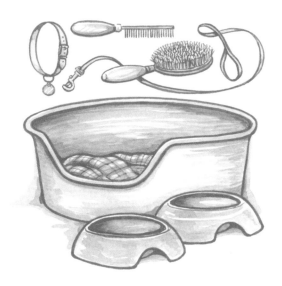

Boxer

Height to shoulder: 53–63 cm (21–25 in)
Weight: About 30 kg (66 lb)
Group: Working

Originally a German breed, the boxer has been recognised for almost a century and is now an extremely popular dog. The breeds that were used as foundation stock are unknown, although the bulldog was certainly one of them. The boxer has a muscular frame and is a large and heavy dog. The coat is fawn or brindle with white markings and should be short and glossy. The most distinctive features of the boxer are its foreshortened muzzle, broad jaw and black mask.

Bred as a guard dog, the boxer is a strong, energetic and active dog that demands a great deal of exercise. A delightful breed with a good nature, it will show great loyalty to an owner and family with plenty of space and plenty of energy but can be distrustful of strangers. It will respond well to firm handling. Its short coat is easy to maintain.

Bull terrier
Height to shoulder: 53–56 cm (21–22 in)
Weight: 24–28 kg (53–62 lb)
Group: Terrier

This is a very courageous and popular breed, although it can be susceptible to deafness. The bull terrier was originally used for fighting and bull-baiting during the eighteenth and nineteenth centuries, and can be seen in old prints in the fighting pits for which it was bred from the bulldog and terrier breeds. The modern dog has changed little in appearance. It is a strong and stocky dog, with a head that appears egg-shaped when viewed from the front. It is usually white, with some tan patches, and the coat is smooth and short.

A rugged dog but a great show-off, the bull terrier can make a good family dog as it is friendly and affectionate, although it needs a firm hand in training as it can tend to be obstinate. Its short coat is easy to maintain.

Bulldog

Height to shoulder: 31–36 cm (12–14 in)
Weight: 22.5–25 kg (50–55 lb)
Group: Utility

One of Britain's national emblems, the bulldog is recognised throughout the world. It is not a big dog, but is a very solid one in every respect, being strong, thick-set, muscular and powerful. The impression it gives of being slow and sluggish is completely contradicted by the great bursts of speed that it can and does produce when the occasion demands. The most outstanding feature of the breed is the head, which is wide and very

wrinkled; the skull is flat and the ears are set well up on the top. The large nose is set right back between the eyes. The front legs are very short and strong, and the chest is wide; the flanks are set high and sloping to the shoulder. Colouring is varied and broken; a broken head marking is considered a very attractive feature in this breed. The coat is short and fine in texture.

Contrary to its appearance, the bulldog is one of the most docile breeds. Its popularity is due to its temperament rather than its looks and build. It can tend to be stubborn, but its loyal nature and bold and courageous behaviour make it particularly good with children or as a protector of any kind.

Cairn terrier

Height to shoulder: 28–31 cm (11–12 in)
Weight: 5.5–6.5 kg (12–14 lb)
Group: Terrier

Among the most popular small dogs, the cairn has lots of spirit and is considered an aristocrat in its own field. It has a small, sharp, foxy head with pricked ears, a compact little body and a tail carried well up. The colouring varies but is usually grey brindle, sometimes with dark points on the ears and muzzle. It was almost certainly bred from the Scottish terrier as the breeds share so many similar features. The cairn has a harsh, weather-resistant double coat that does not require stripping.

The cairn is a game little fellow and its care and maintenance are comparatively trouble-free so it is easy to see why they are so popular. Though likeable and friendly, it makes a good guard dog, as it is alert and intelligent. It makes an ideal companion for a family, fitting in well with any lifestyle.

Chihuahua
Height to shoulder: 15–23 cm (6–9 in)
Weight: 1–1.8 kg (2–4 lb)
Group: Toy

This lively little dog is the smallest breed of dog in the world, and takes its name from the city and state in Mexico from which it originates, where it was sacred to the Aztecs. It has a rounded head with a cheeky expression, large round eyes, and large ears set at a wide angle. The coat can be either short and smooth or long and soft with feathering on the feet and legs, a ruff on the neck and a plume on the tail. Colours vary, but it is usually red (a rich brown) or cream.

This neat, pocket-sized dog is ideal for people with limited space, although probably not the best choice for a family with young children. It makes a good companion for it is brisk, spirited, alert and active. Despite its size, it can be a good guard dog as it will seldom remain quiet if it hears an unusual disturbance. The chihuahua thinks it is a big dog – and at heart it is.

Chow chow

Height to shoulder: 46–56 cm (18–22 in)
Weight: 20–32 kg (44–70 lb)
Group: Utility

The chow's ancestors came from China, where it was kept as a guard dog and also used for hunting. It is unique for its stiff, stilted movement and bluish-black tongue, which makes it unmistakable. It has a lion-like appearance and a medium-sized, compact body. The features are blunt, the eyes oval, and the ears small, thick and slightly rounded. Its beautiful coat comes in

many colours, and can be either rough or smooth. The curled tail is carried well over its back.

The chow is a very dignified dog, friendly once you are familiar with it, which is a good attitude for a dog to guard you and your home. It is extremely loyal to its owner, but it has a tendency to be a one-man dog, which makes it more suitable for an adult household than a busy family. It also likes to be dominant so it is not as tolerant of other animals or children as some other breeds. The rough coat is the more common type, and it needs regular grooming.

Cocker spaniel
Height to shoulder: 38–43 cm (15–17 in)
Weight: 12.75–14.5 kg (28–32 lb)
Group: Gun dog

The cocker spaniel is an extremely popular breed, which is easy to understand as it is a most appealing dog, both in looks and character. Originally from Spain, it was used from the fourteenth century to hunt game birds. It is one of quite a large family that includes the English and Welsh springer, American cocker, field and clumber spaniels, although none of these has reached the popularity of the cocker. A fairly small dog, it has a short back compared to most of its cousins, and is altogether sturdy and compact. The flanks are level with or slightly lower than the back. The neck is long and muscular with sloping shoulders. The most common colourings are red, black and roan; the coat is flat and silky and the legs are well feathered. It has long ears, well covered in long, straight, silky hair.

A medium-sized, attractive dog that makes an excellent companion for both adults and children, the cocker spaniel is a great family pet and fits into the average home well in every way. Its nature is affectionate and kindly, and it has plenty of enthusiasm, with its bustling movement and wagging tail, although it will need firm training to curb its natural exuberance. The owner will also need to spend time keeping the coat in good condition, however, as this will need more grooming than that of a short-coated dog.

Collie, rough and smooth
Height to shoulder: 51–61 cm (20–24 in)
Weight: 18–30 kg (40–66 lb)
Group: Pastoral

The rough collie is and always has been a very exclusive breed. It is a very attractive dog but really it is a worker, not just a pretty face! The two outstanding points of the breed are the head and the coat. The head is very long and graceful in appearance. The skull is flat and tapers to the nose, with small, semi-erect ears and dark brown, almond-shaped eyes that give it a sweet expression. The thick, long coat is in several shades of attractive colouring, including fawn and white, sable (dark brown) and white, and tricolour (black, brown and white). The outer coat is straight and harsh over a soft and furry undercoat. The body is long, arching slightly to the loins, with a deep chest. Collies are friendly and intelligent dogs that love human company, but they are quite large so they will not fit easily into every home. It is a devoted and loyal companion and is extremely faithful, with a gentle temperament. It is intelligent and, therefore, easy to train but it does need a good deal of exercise as it likes to be active and energetic and can be quite vocal. The coat needs a lot of attention to look its best.

The smooth collie is similar in every way apart, of course, from the coat, which is flat and rather harsh, with a very dense undercoat. Colours are similar, although there tends to be more blue merle in the mix. The breeds are now classified separately, although they used to be registered as the same breed.

Corgi *see* Welsh corgi

Dachshund, smooth-haired and long-haired

Height to shoulder: 31–36 cm (12–14 in)
Weight: 9–12 kg (20–26 lb)
Group: Hound

Another dog of German origin that has found its way to Britain and nearly to the top of the tree in favour, this breed was originally introduced and made popular by Queen Victoria and Prince Albert. At that time it was still a sporting breed in Germany, and it certainly has all the attributes of a sporting dog, although it has never been really used in that capacity in Britain. Smooth-haired dachshunds have been used for a variety of jobs over many years and the different demands have resulted in six varieties, of different coats and sizes, including a miniature version. Its long body and deep chest make the breed very distinctive, as do its very short front legs with the elbows well tucked in to the chest. The head has a sharp appearance and tapers to the nose. The short, smooth coat is usually brown (known as red) or black and tan in colour. The tail should be set on fairly high and be strong and tapering, not too long or too curved. It should be carried so that it continues the line of the body.

Altogether most attractive and likeable little dogs, dachshunds have wonderful characters and make excellent house dogs, with a penetrating bark that can be used very effectively against intruders. It is easy to see why they are so popular, as they are small, intelligent, faithful, compact and trouble-free, and cost little to maintain. They are ideal where space is limited and although they can enjoy a great deal of exercise, this is not absolutely necessary to their well-being. However, firmness is needed in their early training as they can be very independent.

The long-haired dachshund is slightly lighter in weight, but the only real difference is in the attractive long, silky coat that lies close to the body, with leg and tail feathers.

Dalmatian

Height to shoulder: 56–61 cm (22–24 in)
Weight: 23–25 kg (51–55 lb)
Group: Utility

This breed – sometimes known as 'plum pudding' dogs – lost their original vocation when people gave up their grand carriages, as it was thought fashionable in the nineteenth century to have a dalmatian running alongside your carriage. However, they have regained their popularity and now appear on the top 20 breeds registered with The Kennel Club. They have similar body features to those found in all sporting breeds.

The legs must be quite straight and the hind legs carry a lot of muscle; the feet are round and hard and consequently able to take a lot of exercise. The head is of moderate length, the skull flat and broad between the ears; the ears are medium-sized and carried high. Markings are important, particularly in show dogs: the spots should be round and clear and distinct from one another. The coat is hard, dense and glossy.

Dalmatians make excellent guard dogs, having a very deep voice that they use readily; their coats are short and easily kept clean and they generally behave very well in the home, being friendly and outgoing. They make great companions, although they need a great deal of exercise. If they are kept cooped up too much, they may become bored and destructive.

Dandie Dinmont terrier

Height to shoulder: 20–28 cm (8–11 in)
Weight: 8–11 kg (18–24 lb)
Group: Terrier

The Dandie Dinmont is a unique-looking dog, and gives the appearance of having a head far too big for its comparatively small body. It has a similar appearance to the better-known sealyham and Scottish terriers. The coat is outstanding and consists of soft, silky hair, which is bunched on the top of the head, giving the somewhat unusual appearance. The jaws are very strong, as the breed was originally used to hunt badgers

and otters, but it is now more popular in the show ring or as a pet. The body is long and curved over the loins, and the tail curves slightly upwards. They are powerfully built for such small dogs. The colouring – called pepper or mustard – is usually bluish-grey or silver-grey, although it is sometimes fawn or light brown. The weatherproof double coat is soft and fluffy (correctly termed 'linty') underneath with a harder topcoat.

If you are looking for a small breed, the Dandie might well be your choice if you require a small, determined and affectionate dog that could melt the hardest of hearts with its soulful expression. It will make a loyal friend and a good guard dog. Although active, it does not require a huge amount of exercise, but it does demand a lot of time spent maintaining the coat in good condition.

Deerhound

Height to shoulder: 71–76 cm (28–30 in)
Weight: 40–45.5 kg (88–100 lb)
Group: Hound

This large, dignified and aristocratic-looking dog was bred with the strength and speed needed to chase and fell deer in the Scottish Highlands. The coat is harsh and weather-resistant, and can be a variety of colours, officially blue-grey, sandy-red, red, fawn or brindle (a streaked, tawny brown). It is wiry and strong, rather than powerfully built, with a long body and legs.

The deerhound is an intelligent and loyal dog, whose true environment really ought to be running about the grounds of an extensive estate, or stretched in front of the fire in a baronial hall. Despite its large size, it is a highly obedient dog that is easy to train, and is always gentle and sociable, but it will require a great deal of exercise.

Dobermann

Height to shoulder: 65–69 cm (25½–27 in)
Weight: Up to 50 kg (110 lb) –
  not stated in breed standard
Group: Working

Bred as a guard dog in Germany, this large, strongly built dog has a well-set and muscular body. The short, smooth, dense coat should be highly glossy; the colours are black, brown, blue or fawn with rust-red markings. It is a powerful dog, quick and alert in its movements, and demands a lot of exercise.

Dobermanns are extremely intelligent, loyal and obedient, but they do need very firm training. Because of their size and demand for plenty of regular exercise, they are particularly suitable as country dogs, although they have a very adaptable outlook to life and can fit into a family very well as long as they receive thorough training and lots of activity. The short coat demands very little attention.

Elkhound

Height to shoulder: 49–52 cm (19½–20½ in)
Weight: 20–23 kg (44–51 lb)
Group: Hound

This is a hardy sporting dog, bred, not surprisingly, for hunting elk across frozen woodlands, and so has strong hunting instincts. Its body is compact and proportionately short, with firm, straight and powerful legs; the hind legs should look straight when viewed from behind. The elkhound has a broad head, moderately long muzzle and pricked ears, set high. The tail is also set high, and tightly curled over the back. The double, weatherproof coat is thick and abundant but not bristly, and it

has a ruff around the neck. The hair is coarse, thick and close. In colour it can be various greys, with black tips to the long outer coat; colouring that is too light or too dark, and pronounced markings on legs and paws are not good for showing.

An elkhound is a bold and lively dog and would enjoy being with an active family but would not be content to live a quiet life if the owners are less energetic. They must not be allowed to become too lazy, or they can tend to put on excess weight. Although the coat is thick, it is not difficult to care for.

English setter

Height to shoulder: 61–69 cm (24–27 in)
Weight: 25–30 kg (55–66 lb)
Group: Gun dog

This beautiful relative of the spaniel makes both an excellent gun dog and a good companion. It is built for running and for doing a long day's work, so the feet are close and compact, with hair between the toes. The head is long and lean, the skull oval between the ears, with plenty of 'brain room'. The dark hazel eyes – bright, mild and intelligent – are a good pointer to the dog's character. The ears are of moderate length, set low on the head, and hang in folds close to the cheeks. The tail is carried almost on a line with the back. The long and silky coat is slightly wavy, and there is plenty of feather on legs and tail. Colour varies but is generally black and white (blue belton), orange and white (orange belton) or lemon and white (lemon belton).

The English setter makes an excellent pet as it is particularly affectionate and thrives on human company. It is responsive and easy to train, and although the coat does require regular attention, it is not difficult to keep in good condition.

English springer spaniel

Height to shoulder: About 53 cm (21 in)
Weight: 22–24 kg (48–53 lb)
Group: Gun dog

This breed is related to the cocker spaniel, but is slightly larger and heavier. Bred as a gun dog, it has been recognised for almost 200 years and is one of the oldest sporting gun dogs. It is a powerfully built, compact dog with a long muscular neck and broad muzzle. The weatherproof coat is straight, usually liver (dark brown) and white but sometimes black and white or tricolour (black, brown and white).

The English springer is a strong, active and intelligent dog, a good companion and therefore an ideal pet. Like so many of the

gun dog breeds, its cheerful, extrovert nature has endeared it to the general public and it is in great demand as an energetic companion for a growing family. A friendly and happy dog, as long as it is kept active and not allowed to become bored, it is relatively easy to groom and amenable to training.

The Welsh springer spaniel is a slightly lighter, smaller dog with a longer, less broad muzzle and short ears. As a gun dog, it is lively, active and tireless.

Field spaniel
Height to shoulder: About 46 cm (18 in)
Weight: 18–25 kg (40–55 lb)
Group: Gun dog

The field spaniel was recognised as a separate breed from the cocker spaniel in 1892, but is much less popular than the cocker. It is a strong, compact dog, bred with plenty of stamina for an active life. The coat is generally brown, or black and roan, and is thick and glossy. The ears are long and oval, and the dark, almond-shaped eyes give a docile expression.

The field spaniel's home is really in the country rather than the town. It is a quiet, sensitive and affectionate dog, although not a popular breed by modern standards. However, it makes an excellent companion and is good with children.

Fox terrier, wire and smooth
Height to shoulder: 36–39.5 cm (14–15½ in)
Weight: 7–8 kg (15½–18 lb)
Group: Terrier

The only outstanding difference between these two breeds is the coat. The wire fox terrier has a very dense and wiry coat, which needs stripping regularly. The smooth fox terrier's coat is also dense but straight and flat. From a show point of view, the coat is considered a very important point. This terrier should have a fairly long head and a good square jaw, which may be shown off to perfection when he has been trimmed and groomed, with the beard left intact. The small ears fold neatly over, close to the cheeks. These are very popular little dogs, bold and game for anything. Their colouring is attractive and usually has a white background with black or tan markings.

The wire fox terrier may be a great companion and house dog, as it is energetic, alert and lively. It is a good choice for family life in town or, properly controlled, in the country. They are noisy and independent little characters, however, and they need stimulation and firm training to learn to get on well with other dogs.

Foxhound

Height to shoulder: 58–63 cm (23–25 in)
Weight: 25–34 kg (55–75 lb)
Group: Hound

This is essentially a hunting dog and is not often found in ordinary households as it needs a considerable amount of food and exercise to keep it in good condition. English foxhounds have been widely exported, and there is an American Foxhound Club. The colour is usually described as hound marked, which means a white background with broken markings of different

shades of brown, including lemon and liver. A very strong-looking dog, it has a square muzzle and sharp brown or hazel eyes and a smooth, weatherproof coat.

This is not really a family dog, as it needs to work to keep it healthy, and it has natural stamina and strength for hunting across country. It is, however, an intelligent and friendly dog, which can be well trained to its job.

German shepherd dog

Height to shoulder: 58–63 cm (23–25 in)
Weight: 34–43 kg (75–95 lb)
Group: Pastoral

This breed is among the six most popular dogs in Britain and is arguably the most popular breed world-wide. It hails from Alsace in Germany, which gives it its alternative name, the Alsatian. Although the German shepherd has the appearance of a wolf, there is no breed connection of any kind. In a way its appearance has sometimes been a handicap as, quite wrongly, many people have made this visual connection and consequently been wary of the dog's temperament. This is certainly one of the most intelligent breeds and can be trained to all kinds of tasks, including working with the Armed forces, as police dogs, as guard dogs in the industrial world, and as guide dogs for the blind. The frame is built in such a way as to ensure an easy movement, which is almost cat-like; the chest is deep, allowing plenty of room for the heart and lungs. The head is long and clean-cut, giving it an extremely sharp and intelligent look. These dogs have very acute hearing and sense of smell. The ears stand erect, and the eyes are almond-shaped and dark. The legs are perfectly straight, and the dog has big bone formation. Colours vary considerably, but among the most common are black and tan, sable (dark brown), grey, fawn and black. There are also white German shepherds, but this colouring is considered highly undesirable in the show ring. The coat is firm and straight with a thick undercoat.

Loyalty, self-assurance, even temper and intelligence combine to make the German shepherd a great companion. It may be wary of other dogs and children, however, but with training and reassurance will become an excellent family dog. Quite a large dog, it does need a fair amount of space and exercise, but grooming is minimal.

Golden retriever *see* Retriever, golden

Gordon setter
Height to shoulder: 62– 66 cm (24½–26 in)
Weight: 25.5–29.5 kg (56–65 lb)
Group: Gun dog

The Gordon setter was originally bred by the Dukes of Gordon for hunting grouse on the Scottish moors, so this dog is powerfully built with plenty of stamina. About the same height as the English setter, the Gordon setter has a muscular body and a thick neck; the skull and muzzle are broad and the eyes are dark and gentle in expression. The wavy black and tan coat is silky and lies flat to the body with feathers on the legs and tail, which is carried almost on a line with the back.

The Gordon setter makes a delightful companion as it is intelligent, gentle, loyal and hard working. Provided it has adequate space and exercise, the Gordon has an excellent, kindly temperament, although it can occasionally be over-exuberant and display somewhat 'daffy' behaviour.

Great Dane
Height to shoulder: 71–76 cm (28–30 in) or more
Weight: 45.5–55 kg (100–120 lb)
Group: Working

A very large breed with a striking appearance, the Great Dane cannot be confused with any other dog. It actually originates in Germany, where it was originally bred to hunt boar and stags. Although it stands very high, it is powerfully strong. The legs are straight and the hindquarters carry plenty of muscle. The head is long and the jaws massive; the ears are medium and set high and the neck is long and arched. There are a variety of colourings including brindle (streaky brown), black, fawn and blue (a slatey grey), harlequin (white with black and blue patches) and the coat is short, dense and sleek.

The Great Dane is very amenable to training when young. It is an intelligent and kindly dog, quite sociable in nature, so it will make a friendly, outgoing companion and a good guard dog. Of course, it goes without saying that it is only an appropriate choice for someone with plenty of space.

Greyhound

Height to shoulder: 69–76 cm (27–30 in)
Weight: 27–32 kg (60–70 lb)
Group: Hound

Primarily a sporting and racing dog, the greyhound has a good, deep chest and oblique shoulder blades. The hindquarters are strong and broad and the hind legs are muscular and wide apart. A dog for showing should have forelegs that are short from knee to ground and hind legs that are short from hock to ground,

with the length in the upper part of the leg. The tail is long, tapering and nicely curved. The coat is fine, thick and close, and there is a great variety of colours, including black, blue (slatey grey), brindle (streaked brown), white and a mixture of any of these (known as 'particoloured'), the majority of dogs having some white markings. Greyhounds have been accepted for many centuries as one of the most graceful of all breeds, elegant but full of muscular power.

Greyhounds that have retired from the race-track make excellent family companions. They are intelligent, gentle, affectionate and even-tempered, requiring less exercise than one might imagine. The coat is easy to care for. Space is required, however, as this is a fairly large dog.

Irish setter
Height to shoulder: 57–66 cm (22½–26 in)
Weight: 27–32 kg (60–70 lb)
Group: Gun dog

This breed must rank among the most glamorous of all the
breeds of dog. The most distinctive characteristic of this
beautiful dog is the colour, which should be a rich, deep
chestnut. It may have white on the chest, throat or toes, a small
star on the forehead, or a narrow blaze on the nose or face, but
this is not desirable for show purposes. Otherwise it closely
resembles its cousins, the English and Gordon setters.

The medium- to dark-coloured eyes of the Irish setter have a soft expression, which is a good indication of its sweet, affectionate and fun-loving temperament. Highly intelligent and easy to train, its air of devil-may-care is totally genuine and its friendly nature makes it a good household dog, ready for all the fun an active family can give.

Irish terrier

Height to shoulder: 46– 48 cm (18–19 in)
Weight: 11–12 kg (24–26 lb)
Group: Terrier

The Irish terrier is well known as being a very brave little dog. It is slightly heavier than a fox terrier, but similar in many ways. Its colouring is usually of a reddish tan but is sometimes wheaten red; it has a short, hard, wiry coat, which does not require a lot of attention beyond a good regular brushing with a stiff brush. The stance is very upright and the front legs are straight. The neck is inclined to be long; the skull is flat and the ears are V-shaped.

The Irish terrier is well worth considering among the smaller dogs, particularly if you are looking for a good guard and companion. It is loyal and intelligent and, although noisy and occasionally over-enthusiastic, it is always responsive to training. While it has a very strong character, it makes a perfect companion and house pet. Daredevils at heart, they can be reckless or even foolhardy where other canines are concerned, but have the most gentle and loving disposition coupled with a delightful sense of humour.

Irish water spaniel
Height to shoulder: 51–58 cm (20–23 in)
Weight: 20–30 kg (44–66 lb)
Group: Gun dog

This delightful-looking dog, the tallest of the spaniels, is distinguishable by its unusual coat, which is long and curly with a curly topknot and a smooth face and tail. As the name suggests, this hunting dog was used to retrieve water fowl, so its coat is water-resistant. The colour of the coat should be a rich liver. The dog has a powerful frame, and is enthusiastic and strongly built.

The water spaniel needs a great deal of exercise and can become boisterous if its lifestyle is not sufficiently active, so it is most suited to a life in the country. It loves swimming, and this makes the coat easier to groom, which is fortunate as this is essential and always time-consuming. Although it has a stable and affectionate nature, it is therefore not the first choice for most families.

Irish wolfhound

Height to shoulder: 71–79 cm (28–31 in)
Weight: 50–55 kg (110–120 lb)
Group: Hound

This is the tallest of all dogs, very muscular, strong but graceful, easy in movement, powerful and fast, and of commanding appearance. The forelegs must be straight. The head and neck are carried high, the neck is long and well arched, without any loose skin about the throat, while the ears should be carried like those of the greyhound, not hanging flat to the face. The muzzle is long and fairly pointed and the skull not too broad. The tail has an upward sweep and a slight curve towards the end. The hair is very rough and wiry, long over the eyes and under the jaw. Colours include grey, brindle (streaked brown), red (rich brown), black, pure white and fawn.

A delightful dog with a warm and friendly character, this is not a dog to be taken on lightly because of its tremendous size. It needs a lot of exercise, plenty of space and large quantities of high-quality food. Very much a country dog.

Jack Russell terrier

Height to shoulder: About 25–31 cm (10–12 in)
Weight: About 6 kg (13 lb)
Group: n/a

Although very popular in the UK, the Jack Russell terrier is not yet recognised by The Kennel Club, although it does recognise the Parson Russell Terrier, which is a very similar breed. Small, active and strong, the breed was developed in the late nineteenth century as a ratter and to work fox. It is a small dog

with a strong frame and fairly short, strong, muscular legs. The head is quite wide and small, with almond-shaped, deep-set eyes and small, V-shaped ears carried close to the head. The coat is naturally harsh and dense, and can be rough or smooth. It is usually white, or white with tan, lemon or black markings, usually on the head and tail.

An alert and feisty little dog, strong and full of stamina and enthusiasm, the Jack Russell is a bold and friendly breed that can make a good house dog. It needs to be active, however, as it is not a dog that enjoys a lazy life, and must be given very firm training so that it does not become over-exuberant.

Keeshond
Height to shoulder: 43–46 cm (17–18 in)
Weight: 25–30 kg (55–66 lb)
Group: Utility

This breed shares a title with the more unusual schipperke, both being known as Dutch barge dogs. The keeshond is a most attractive animal: compact in size and with a very foxy appearance, pricked ears and alert features. It is of medium build and has a thick, bushy coat of a sable (dark brown)

colouring or wolf marking; the muzzle, legs and tail are of a slightly lighter shade. The ears are erect, and the breed is very sensitive to the slightest sound; this makes them excellent guard dogs and they are used for this express purpose on the canals, for protecting barges and their contents.

Quite a popular dog in Britain, it will give a great deal of companionship to all ages as it is of moderate size, confident, friendly and intelligent. The coat does require a good deal of grooming to keep it in good condition.

Kerry blue terrier
Height to shoulder: 46–48 cm (18–19 in)
Weight: 15–17 kg (33–37 lb)
Group: Terrier

This breed has gained great prominence during the past 20 years, although it is still not as popular as some of the other terriers. The strong point of the Kerry blue is its coat: it is usually dark grey in colour, sometimes various related shades, and on occasions appears almost black. It is very soft in texture, with an attractive fringe over the eyes. The dog has a very solid build, with strong, muscular legs; the body is of medium length and level. The head is long and the jaw very strong.

An alert and fearless watchdog, the Kerry blue is an ideal house guard and companion. They make good family dogs but, like all terriers, need firm handling and sound training. They also need a moderate amount of exercise. The coat requires regular trimming to keep it in good condition.

King Charles spaniel

Height to shoulder: 25–28 cm (10–11 in)
Weight: 3.5–6 kg (8–13 lb)
Group: Toy

As the name indicates, this breed goes back to the period of Charles II, when these dogs were the King's firm favourites. The most popular colourings are black and tan, and tricolour (a background of white with patches of black and tan) but they can also be ruby (rich, reddish brown) and Blenheim (rich brown and white). This is a small spaniel and should be low to the ground, with a large, well-domed skull. Its nose is short and

turned up and its ears are long and hang low, carrying long hair. Its eyes are large, dark and set wide apart and its jaw is slightly undershot. The coat is long and silky and has the same feathering as the others of the spaniel family.

This happy and intelligent dog looks every bit the aristocrat. It will suit the connoisseur well and yet will make the perfect family pet, as it is both elegant and cheerful and makes a very affectionate companion. Although long, the coat is not difficult to maintain, and as it is a small dog it does not require much space or exercise.

Labrador *see* **Retriever, labrador**

Lhasa apso

Height to shoulder: About 25 cm (10 in)
Weight: 4.5–8 kg (10–18 lb)
Group: Utility

The lhasa apso has become more popular recently, especially for showing, not least because of its long, heavy coat, which comes in a huge variety of colours, including browns – golden, sandy, honey and dark grizzle (grey/brown) – greys – slate and smoke – black, white, brown, and even a mixture (particolour). It has a long fringe, beard and whiskers. The skull is quite narrow, and the face is straight with dark eyes and heavily feathered ears. The legs are straight, and the body should be well balanced and compact. The tail is erect and carried well over the back.

Alert and even-tempered, the lhasa apso can be inclined to be aloof with strangers, although it is generally a happy and confident dog. The coat, which needs a great deal of attention, is the crucial factor when it comes to choosing this dog; its owner must be someone with plenty of time and patience.

Manchester terrier
Height to shoulder: 38–41 cm (15–16 in)
Weight: 5–10 kg (11–22 lb)
Group: Terrier

The Manchester terrier gained its name from its popularity as a ratter in that area of Britain, both in the countryside and also in the dog ring, where the men used to gamble on the number of rats their dog could kill in a given time. It has a smooth, short, naturally glossy coat that is easy to maintain. The colour is black and rich tan, with a uniform pattern. The head should be long, flat and narrow with tapering jaws; the eyes are small and dark, set fairly close together, and the ears are usually semi-erect. The neck is long and tapers from the shoulders to the head. The body is short and raised slightly at the loins with quite straight and fairly long legs. The tail is carried straight.

Energetic and alert, the Manchester can make a good house dog as it can be loyal and devoted. Its moderate size makes it suitable for many households, while its glossy coat demands very little attention. It is an active and noisy little character, however, that will need a firm hand.

The English toy terrier, or 'black and tan' as it is sometimes called, is a miniature edition of the Manchester terrier. It is a very tiny dog indeed and frequently turns the scales at less than 3 kg (7 lb), being about 25–30 cm (10–12 in) high. Its characteristics are similar to the large breed. It makes an excellent house dog, particularly where space is limited.

Mastiff
Height to shoulder: 70–76 cm (27½–30 in)
Weight: 79–86 kg (175–190 lb)
Group: Working

This dog has a longer history than most of our British breeds, but almost became extinct in Britain after the Second World War. Stock was then imported and since then numbers have risen steadily. The breed was found in Britain by the Romans and many were dispatched back to Rome for fighting in the arena with other animals; they were also used in Britain for bull-baiting. The dog is heavy rather than big in bulk; it has a broad, square head, a short tan coat, small ears, a very broad chest and a powerful body.

A mastiff makes a formidable guard and companion. However, an average home could not accommodate a dog this size, even though it does not require as much exercise as its bulk might indicate. The mastiff is far better suited to the large country home. It is an intelligent dog requiring plenty of human contact – and plenty of good food.

The bull mastiff is often confused with the mastiff, but is actually derived from a cross with the bulldog, though little of the latter shows itself today beyond the head features. The bull mastiff is slightly smaller than the mastiff, at 66–71 cm (26–28 in) at the shoulder, and weighs upwards of 41 kg (90 lb) – a very solid build. The coat is short and usually coloured fawn with a dark mask; the head is square and quite wrinkled and the ears are V-shaped and set well back. The muzzle is square and deep and the whole dog is very muscular with a wide, deep chest. A popular breed but probably not for the average household.

Miniature pinscher

Height to shoulder: 25–31 cm (10–12 in)
Weight: 4–5 kg (9–11 lb)
Group: Toy

The full-sized German pinscher was one of the breeds used as foundation stock for the dobermann, but is now a much less common breed and rarely seen. The miniature pinscher is smart and clean in outline, sturdy and compact in body, and features a unique trotting gait. The smooth coat – black, blue or chocolate with sharply defined tan markings – is short, glossy and, therefore, easy to maintain.

Like the chihuahua, this small dog makes an excellent guard as it has acute hearing and a penetrating bark, which it uses if it detects any unusual disturbance. An energetic and intelligent dog that makes a perfect companion, it has the advantage of its small size, which makes it an ideal choice for smaller homes.

Old English sheepdog

Height to shoulder: 56–61 cm (22–24 in)
Weight: 29.5–30.5 kg (65–67 lb)
Group: Pastoral

This breed, sometimes called the bobtail, epitomises the English way of life in more ways than one, and is an extremely popular breed. The outstanding feature is the coat, which is usually blue-grey in colour and long and shaggy with a waterproof undercoat. The size of the dog does vary, and on the whole the smaller type is used for shepherding and the larger variety for showing. Although the Old English would be described as a big dog, much of this is actually the thick coat. The breed is very hardy and full of energy. The eyes are a dark colour and are seldom visible through the thick hair covering the face; the skull and jaw are square, and the head rather long and narrow. It has solid and straight forelegs with small, round feet, and a short

and compact body. The tail is usually docked. Plenty of these dogs are still used with sheep but they would hardly be recognised against their well-groomed show-ring cousins.

Although a great favourite and with a very high intelligence, this is not a dog for those without plenty of time and patience to exercise it. It requires a lot of attention to look its best, with unlimited grooming. However, it has plenty of stamina, is even tempered, faithful and trustworthy.

Papillon

Height to shoulder: 20–28 cm (8–11 in)
Weight: 4–4.5 kg (9–10 lb)
Group: Toy

This elegant and attractive little French dog has gained in popularity in recent years. The long, silky coat is white with either red or black markings, heavily fringed with a plumed tail. It gets the name from the French word *papillon*, meaning 'butterfly', because of the shape of its ears, which are carried erect and have long, silky fringes.

This is an alert, lively, friendly and energetic dog that loves attention. Regular and careful grooming is essential, but as long as you have time for this, the papillon can make a great little house dog. It is happy, easy to train, and has proved extremely clever in obedience. Its small size puts it on the shortlist as a good choice for many households.

Pekinese
Height to shoulder: 15–23 cm (6–9 in)
Weight: 5–5.5 kg (11–12 lb)
Group: Toy

The pekinese can be traced back to the Tang dynasty in China. It has always made up a very big entry at dog shows, and is a firm favourite. This is an extremely intelligent little dog with a good sense of humour. It also has a very dignified air, which it assumes when the mood takes it. The beauty of the breed lies mainly in the coat, which is thick and long, with profuse feathering on the thighs, legs, tail and feet. It has a heavy mane and a frill under the neck. It has a big head and flat, wrinkled muzzle. The legs are short and the front ones slightly bowed. The tail is carried right over the back. Colouring is varied.

Loyal and fearless, intelligent and easy to keep, the pekinese remains a popular choice, especially for those with a small amount of space or a family that does not want an over-active breed. Regular and thorough grooming, however, is essential.

Pointer

Height to shoulder: 61–69 cm (24–27 in)
Weight: 20–30 kg (44–66 lb)
Group: Gun dog

This is one of larger gun dog breeds, a magnificent dog that is extremely popular in the country, particularly with gamekeepers. It has acute hearing and a keen sense of smell, making it perfect for its work. As its name indicates, it will instinctively 'point' at game, and also knows how to drive game. It has German counterparts, the wire-haired and short-haired

pointers, although, paradoxically, it is thought that these types originally hailed from Spain. The pointer is a very powerful dog with plenty of staying power, which is necessary for field work. The colouring is normally a shade of brown (lemon, orange or liver) or black and white, and the coat is short and glossy. The dog has a long head and neck, the latter being very muscular; the ears are of medium length and set fairly high.

The pointer is not really a domestic dog, being better suited to life on the farm. It has a perfect temperament, and is a great friend of man, but it would be lost without the country.

Pointer, German short-haired
Height to shoulder: 53–63 cm (21–25 in)
Weight: 27–32 kg (60–70 lb)
Group: Gun dog

The short-haired pointer was bred as a gun dog, and it has the usual qualities of a working dog: strong build, stamina, speed and a good nose. It is normally liver (dark brown) and mottled white, like the pointer, but is sometimes solid liver, black or white. The head is broader than the pointer, but the dog shares the muscular neck and powerful build. The coat is short and lies flat to the body.

The short-haired pointer is a good working dog, and is also gentle, affectionate and even-tempered. It combines grace, energy and stamina in a neat frame, but it is perhaps most suited to a working or very active environment.

Pomeranian

Height to shoulder: 22–28 cm (8½–11 in)
Weight: 2.5–3.5 kg (5½–8 lb)
Group: Toy

This breed was at one time the favourite toy dog – Queen Victoria was a devotee – and they are still extremely popular and enjoy a prominent entry at dog shows. When they were first introduced into Britain, they were white in colour and considerably bigger than the present-day specimens, which are related to some of the Scandinavian breeds and have been bred down in size. A number of colours have been introduced by specialists, the usual one being a foxy red, and the coat is long and fluffy with a prominent neck ruff. This is a very neat little dog with a sharp, fox-like appearance and a short body. The small ears are erect, and the tail lies flat over the back and is well covered with long hair. The feet are small and neat. Unusually, the bitches are often slightly larger than the dogs.

This is another breed whose coat requires a great deal of attention to look its best. It is lively, vivacious, sweet-tempered and affectionate, so if you have the time and inclination for plenty of grooming, it can be a good choice for a household pet.

Poodle

Height to shoulder: Over 38 cm (15 in)
Weight: About 19 kg (42 lb)
Group: Utility

The most recognisable feature of the poodle is its curly coat, which is very thick and of a hard texture. It can be clipped into one of several forms although The Kennel Club breed standard recommends the traditional 'lion' clip. Colours vary, including black, white, silver, brown and apricot. It has a rather long, well-shaped head, a long muzzle and fairly long and wide ears.

The head is carried high, and the body is compact and slightly hollowed. The front legs are straight, the feet small, and the tail is carried high and straight.

An intelligent dog, poodles make excellent companions. They are light-hearted, elegant, friendly and high-spirited, with a happy nature, and their sporting and clown-like tendencies make them an ideal family dog.

The miniature poodle is also very popular, and can be easily picked up and tucked under the arm. The characteristics are the same as the standard poodle, but the height is 28–38 cm (11–15 in) and the toy poodle is even smaller, the recognised height being less than 28 cm (11 in). Both these would make a good choice for a more elderly or less energetic owner, or someone with a smaller home.

Pug

Height to shoulder: 25–28 cm (10–11 in)
Weight: 6.5–8 kg (14–18 lb)
Group: Toy

Originally bred in China, the pug was brought to Britain in the seventeenth century, and is now a popular town dog, being small, intelligent, alert and easy to look after. The distinctive feature of the pug is its head, which is large with a foreshortened muzzle, a heavily wrinkled face and large, dark eyes. The mask around the eyes is black while the rest of the coat may be silver, apricot, fawn or black; it is smooth and short and requires very little maintenance. A stocky little dog, the pug has a solid, muscular body, a thick neck and a tightly curled tail.

An adaptable companion, the pug can fit in well with family life, and its small size, even temper, intelligence and lively character make it a good choice for both young and old.

Pyrenean mountain dog

Height to shoulder: 65–70 cm (25½–27½ in)
Weight: 40–50 kg (88–110 lb)
Group: Pastoral

This huge, white dog, one of the largest breeds, is similar in appearance to the St Bernard and does not reach maturity until it is three or four years old. It was originally bred in the Pyrenees to protect sheep from wolves, and is still an excellent guard dog, but needs careful training as it is inclined to be rather independent. The coat is thick and white, sometimes with darker markings of grey or brown, and the legs are feathered. It is solidly built, with a thick neck and large head.

Surprisingly, this dog is not remarkably active – a short walk or a long ramble in the country will suit it equally well. However, this is a very large and powerful breed and does need spacious surroundings and plenty of good-quality food. Its great size makes it unsuitable for most homes in towns.

Retriever, golden
Height to shoulder: 51–61 cm (20–24 in)
Weight: 27–36 kg (60–80 lb)
Group: Gun dog

This is a handsome, powerful dog, highly intelligent and easy to teach, so it is not surprising that it is one of the most popular dogs in the world. The eyes are wide apart, dark and gentle in expression. The forelegs are perfectly straight, the hocks well bent and placed low to the ground. The outer coat is flat or wavy (not curly), and there is feathering on the thighs, tail and forelegs. The colour is any shade of gold or cream.

Retrievers are versatile, good-natured and intelligent. They make wonderful guide dogs, obedience dogs and drugs and explosives detecting dogs – all in addition to the job they do so well, simply being a fun-loving member of the family. Quite large and active, they need a fair amount of exercise and a moderate amount of grooming. A retriever retains its puppyish high spirits until at least two years of age, and always remains kindly and eager to please.

Retriever, labrador

Height to shoulder: 55–57 cm (21½–22½ in)
Weight: 25–34 kg (55–75 lb)
Group: Gun dog

This is the most popular breed in Britain, strongly built, active and with great powers of endurance. It differs in appearance from the golden retriever, as it has a slightly broader head and wider chest. The coat is short, thick and smooth and the colour may be black, yellow or liver (chocolate brown). The jaws are powerful and long, and the wide skull gives plenty of 'brain room'. Eyes are medium sized, brown or hazel.

This dog is a real gentleman. The labrador retriever adores children and has a kind and loving nature, so makes a great pet

for an active family so long as there is enough space for a large dog. Loyal and amenable to training, it is not surprising that this is the choice for so many households. Plenty of exercise will be required or an adult dog, however, as labradors tend to run to fat easily.

Rottweiler

Height to shoulder: 58–69 cm (23–27 in)
Weight: 41–50 kg (90–110 lb)
Group: Working

A working dog originally from Germany, the rottweiler has strong natural guarding instincts and, although it should not be aggressive, it does require a very firm hand in training. It has a powerful body, strong and muscular, with straight front legs.

The eyes are dark and the expression alert. The coat is short and glossy, mainly black with tan markings, including patches on the cheeks, each side of the muzzle and above each eye.

Intelligent and good-natured, the rottweiler has natural guarding instincts, but is not vicious by nature. Extremely strong and imposing, they are easily obedience trained and enjoy working, but this is not a dog for the inexperienced.

Saint Bernard
Height to shoulder: 61–71 cm (24–28 in)
Weight: 50–91 kg (110–200 lb)
Group: Working

This is one of the biggest known breeds and is a very noble and handsome dog. These dogs have been bred at the St Bernard Hospice on the Great St Bernard Pass in Switzerland for some centuries; trained by monks, they have performed many great errands of mercy in saving travellers lost in the snowy wastes of the pass. The dog is not used in any working capacity in Britain, though it is definitely trainable. A good specimen will be well proportioned and big in all respects. A very 'upstanding' dog, it has straight forelegs with large feet. Its head is huge, with a square muzzle, and the colouring is tan or chestnut with white patches on both the body and the head. The coat is thick and flat with some feathering on the legs. While it is among the less common breeds, there are a good number of breeders and

exhibitors in Britain, and the dog always enjoys a prominent place at the big shows.

The St Bernard is a delightful dog, trustworthy, intelligent, courageous and kind, but it is not a cheap proposition. It also takes up a lot of space and anyone thinking about keeping one would do well to 'borrow' an adult dog to see how much space is needed once the new purchase has grown to full size.

Saluki
Height to shoulder: 58–71 cm (23–28 in)
Weight: 15–25 kg (33–55 lb)
Group: Hound

The saluki has grace, energy, speed, strength and endurance. Also known as the gazelle hound, it was originally bred in Arabia for coursing hare and gazelle. The coat is smooth and silky, and the slight feathering on the legs, at the back of the thighs and sometimes on thighs and shoulders, is generally associated with this breed. There is also a completely smooth variety. The head is long and narrow, but the skull is moderately broad between the ears; the nose is black or liver-coloured (dark brown). The forelegs are straight and long from elbow to knee; the hindquarters are strong, with the hip bones wide apart, and hocks low to the ground. The dog is built for running and jumping. The tail is long, set low, and carried in a curve.

This is a dog that needs a home in the country and plenty of human contact, as it easily becomes bored if left alone. It is a very intelligent and sensitive breed, and extremely affectionate with those it loves, although it can be reserved with strangers.

Samoyed

Height to shoulder: 46–56 cm (18–22 in)
Weight: 22.5–30 kg (50–66 lb)
Group: Pastoral

The samoyed is a popular dog because of its striking appearance and affectionate nature. It is a large, heavy dog, built for speed and stamina as a sled or herding dog. Although the coat looks silky, it is in fact thick and coarse with a soft undercoat, designed to protect the dogs from the weather in Russia where they were used to herd reindeer. The tail is thick and curled, the forelegs straight and feathered, and the dog has a thick ruff round the neck. The coat is white, cream or biscuit-coloured.

A large and strong dog, the samoyed needs a good deal of exercise and must be groomed regularly and thoroughly. They are affectionate, good with children and love to play, being especially fond of a romp in the snow. The Sammy, as it is often called, has a smiling expression and looks on the world as something to be enjoyed, and is alert and active. It does, however, tend to bark a lot.

Schnauzer

Height to shoulder: 46– 48 cm (18–19 in)
Weight: 14.5–15.5 kg (32–34 lb)
Group: Utility

The schnauzer is a thick-set and muscular dog with straight forelegs, a thick, straight neck and a characteristic square muzzle with long whiskers. The ears are V-shaped, set high and drooping forwards. The most common colouring is grey (often called salt and pepper) with some black or white markings, but black is also popular. The schnauzer looks its best when professionally trimmed, and the slightly coarse, wiry coat is then easy to maintain. The unusual appearance of the schnauzer, with its attractive long eyebrows and whiskers, as well as its intelligent nature make this increasingly popular dog a great companion, and the miniature schnauzer is listed in the top 20 breeds registered with The Kennel Club.

The schnauzer could find a good home with an active and energetic family who have enough time and patience to give this strong and vigorous dog enough exercise and keep its coat in the best condition. The beard and legs need to be washed regularly, but otherwise it seldom needs bathing.

The miniature schnauzer is a high-spirited, companionable little dog, which is ideal for the smaller home as it is less than 36 cm (14 in) high, lively, affectionate and easy to look after. Intelligent and simple to train, it has a penetrating bark that makes it a good guard dog.

Scottish terrier

Height to shoulder: 25–28 cm (10–11 in)
Weight: 8.5–10.5 kg (19–23 lb)
Group: Terrier

The Scottish terrier, or Aberdeen as it is sometimes known, is popular the world over. A game little dog and very solidly built, it has short legs, a long head and strong jaw. The ears are small and erect; the neck is short and thick-set. The tail is not docked.

The Scottie has a short, hard, wiry coat, which is usually black in colour, although it may also be wheaten (light brown) or brindle (streaked brown).

The Scottish terrier is energetic and outgoing and makes a fine little house dog in every way. It is keen, loyal and independent and likes to be kept busy, but it needs little grooming and its size means that it is easy to keep well exercised and healthy. The coat requires regular stripping, however. It is a great sportsman and afraid of nothing, and is certainly among the most popular breeds in the dog world.

Sealyham
Height to shoulder: 25–31 cm (10–12 in)
Weight: 8–9 kg (18–20 lb)
Group: Terrier

The sealyham is a very game little dog, supple, active and ready to romp and play. They are mostly white in colour, usually with a lemon or brown patch on the head or on the back and ears.

The top coat is long and hard, while the undercoat is soft and weather-resistant. The body is low and thick-set, with a broad, deep chest, and the legs are very short. The head is fairly wide, and the jaws powerful; the neck is long and thick. The dog is certainly well built for its original task of digging out vermin. It is a great sport and very tenacious, and considering its very short legs can stand a great deal of exercise.

It is possibly the sealyham's enthusiasm that appeals to so many dog lovers and it is well worth considering if you have a modest-sized house and a large garden. It can be just as much at home in the town or the country and makes a good family pet, although it can be quite vocal. The coat does require regular stripping.

Shetland sheepdog

Height to shoulder: 36–37 cm (14–14½ in)
Weight: 6–7 kg (13–15½ lb)
Group: Pastoral

This is a very popular breed of dog. One would seldom expect to use the word 'pretty' to describe a working dog, but it certainly applies to the Sheltie. In the isles of their origin, they are of a rougher type, and are used solely for working. Their intelligence is outstanding. The coat should be long with a generous frill, and the colouring is usually sable and white, though there are many other colours. The legs are feathered and the tail carried down with an upward curl at the tip; the skull is flat, the nose long and the eyes are almond-shaped and brown in colour; ears are small and carried half-erect. This dog has a deep chest and straight forelegs. Despite its appearance, it is very hardy and tough.

The Shetland's alert, gentle and intelligent nature makes it a good house dog and it is easy to train. It is responsive to its owners but a little reserved with strangers. The coat does demand regular grooming, although it is not difficult to care for.

Shih tzu

Height to shoulder: Up to 27 cm (10½ in)
Weight: 4.5–8 kg (10–18 lb)
Group: Utility

A sturdy little dog with a broad, round head and widely spaced eyes, the shih tzu has a beard and whiskers, with the hair growing upwards, so that, according to some people, it resembles a chrysanthemum. The coat is long and dense, with a good undercoat, and there is a range of colours. It has a square, short, slightly upturned muzzle. The eyes are dark and the ears are long and drooping. It has a sturdy and broad chest and short, straight legs with an abundance of hair. The heavily plumed tail is set high and carried well over the back.

An intelligent and active dog, the shih tzu is independent and sociable and has become very popular recently. Its coat demands a great deal of attention to look its best but it is a delightful companion, happy to be part of a family.

Skye terrier

Height to shoulder: 23–25 cm (9–10 in)
Weight: 8.5–10.5 kg (19–23 lb)
Group: Terrier

One of the oldest Scottish breeds, the Skye terrier is very much an individual dog. Its great feature is its coat, which is very long and flat, and covers the forehead and eyes, with a feathered tail. The body is long and low, and the back is level, with a very slight drop from the flanks to the shoulder. The ears are usually pricked, though they may be long and pendulant; the head is long and the skull fairly wide.

The Skye terrier has a very strong bark for such a small dog, and will certainly let you know if there is anyone about, making it a good guard dog. A one-man dog, it tends to be distrustful of strangers but is devoted and loyal to family and friends.

Springer spaniel *see* English springer spaniel

Weimaraner

Height to shoulder: 56–69 cm (22–27 in)
Weight: 32–39 kg (70–86 lb)
Group: Gun dog

The weimaraner is a real aristocrat of the dog world. The German ruling class who originally bred these dogs for hunting game birds wanted an exclusive-looking breed that also had all the best qualities of the sporting breeds. This superb, tall dog with its silver grey coat was the result. It is a large, strong dog with straight forelegs, large ears and pale blue-grey or amber eyes. Some dogs have small white markings on the chest, but any other markings are not desirable if the dog is intended for show purposes.

The weimaraner is one of the top 20 breeds registered with The Kennel Club. It is fearless, friendly, protective and obedient but it does need space and exercise, and must be properly trained by a firm handler. It does not require special grooming.

Welsh corgi

Height to shoulder: 31 cm (12 in)
Weight: 10–12 kg (22–26 lb)
Group: Pastoral

There are two varieties of corgi, the Cardigan and the Pembroke, both of which were used extensively for herding cattle in their native counties, keeping the animals moving by nipping them in the hocks. The corgi is a stocky little dog with short legs; the chest is broad and deep, the body fairly long and the tail short and stumpy. It has a sharp appearance with a slightly tapering muzzle, the skull being wide between the ears and the ears carried erect. This dog has a very foxy appearance and the hard-textured coat is short and thick, usually red in colour or red and white, but it can be sable, fawn or black and tan. The Cardigan is thought to be the older of the two breeds, the main difference being its long tail, rather like a fox's brush, which should be set in line with the body.

The corgi is a great present-day favourite. The British Royal Family, especially Queen Elizabeth II, have been greatly instrumental in this little dog's popularity but it is probably also very much due to the way they fit into the average family with little or no trouble. They are outgoing and bold, with a practical outlook, and are easy to care for, alert and enthusiastic.

Welsh terrier
Height to shoulder: 37–39 cm (14½–15½ in)
Weight: 9–9.5 kg (20–21 lb)
Group: Terrier

The Welsh terrier could be described as the miniature Airedale. In size, it compares with the fox terrier. The coat is very wiry and is usually black and tan in colour. The Welsh terrier has a flat, rather wide head with a powerful jaw, small, V-shaped ears carried high, and small eyes. This dog is fairly wide for its size, with a short back, straight front legs and small feet.

This breed is an ideal dog for the average home, being a good companion and economical to maintain. It needs periodical trimming, but otherwise is relatively easy to look after. It is good with children, and has a happy and affectionate character with a cheerful, energetic spirit.

West Highland white terrier

Height to shoulder: 28 cm (11 in)
Weight: 7–10 kg (15½–22 lb)
Group: Terrier

This breed is the highest-placed terrier in the list of the top 20 breeds registered with The Kennel Club. It is a delightful little dog, completely white in colour, and much the same size as the cairn terrier. It is stockily built, with a deep chest, straight back and plenty of muscle. It is a very strong little dog, originally bred for ratting and seeking out other small vermin. Its head is thickly coated with hair, and it has powerful jaws, small pricked ears, and a tail that should be about 15 cm (6 in) long. The legs are short, with the upper parts bent and set under the body. The coat is hard and of medium length, with a long outer coat over a short, soft undercoat; although it should be pure white, it sometimes has a creamy colouring.

The West Highland is a very sharp little dog for the home and a good companion. It is even-tempered, loves company and responds well to training. It really is an excellent all-purpose pet. The coat requires regular grooming.

Whippet
Height to shoulder: 44–51 cm (17½–20 in)
Weight: 12.5–14 kg (27–31 lb)
Group: Hound

This dog enjoys outstanding popularity, particularly in the north of England, where racing is popular. It is built for speed, with long legs and strong and broad hindquarters. The tops of the shoulder blades should be fairly close together. The head is long and lean, flat at the top and rather wide between the eyes. The chest should be deep, with plenty of 'heart room'. The long tapering tail should not be carried higher than the level of the back when the dog is in action. The eyes are bright, alert and fiery and the ears are small, fine in texture, and are carried half erect, not bolt upright. Colours are very varied – they may be black, blue (slate grey), red (rich brown), fawn, brindle (streaked brown), white or mixtures of these.

Affectionate, gentle and easy to manage, the whippet makes an ideal dog for the home. The coat requires no special grooming, and its medium size means it is suitable for many smaller households.

Yorkshire terrier

Height to shoulder: 23–25 cm (9–10 in)
Weight: About 3 kg (7 lb)
Group: Toy

A very popular little dog, the Yorkshire terrier's long coat is its most outstanding feature. It hangs evenly down each side of the body with a parting in the centre from nose to tail. The hair should be fine and glossy and dark steel grey in colour, with a

rich tan head and similar leg and chest markings. The puppies are actually born black and tan, and change colour after a few months. The body is compact and level, legs straight and hairy, feet round, and the tail may be docked to medium length. The head is small and rather flat, and the muzzle of medium length.

The Yorkshire terrier is an ideal dog for the elderly person with limited accommodation, as it is not only a great companion, but also very sharp-witted with a keen sense of hearing. Despite its diminutive size, the Yorkshire terrier can hold its own with considerably larger breeds. It has a very strong character for such a tiny dog and is very much liked as a house pet, being small enough to curl easily into one's lap. The long coat needs a great deal of grooming right from birth; as the hair grows after the first few months, it has to be kept oiled.

Chapter 4
Your Blueprint for the Perfect Dog

Use this chapter to narrow down your choice of the ideal dog for you and your family. Fill in the blanks, cross out the breeds that are not suitable, and make a short list of choices before you start to home in on the perfect selection.

Owner's profile

Think about yourself and your family as dog owners. Then when you come to consider each breed, look at your answers and compare them with the dog's characteristics and needs.

Why do you want a dog? . . . .

How big is your house? . . . .

How big is the garden? . . . .

Are you fussy about keeping the house tidy? . . . .

How much time do you have available
  each day for walks? . . . .

How many children do you have? . . . .

How old are they? . . . .

Where will the dog be in the family hierarchy? . . . .

Who will take the main responsibility
   for the dog's care? . . . .

How will the children be involved in the
   dog's care? . . . .

Does your family have any special needs?
   (For example, allergies, babies, frail elderly relatives)
   . . . .

Where will the dog live in the house? . . . .

Are there any other pets? . . . .

What is your maximum budget for buying the dog? . . . .

What weekly maintenance budget can you afford? . . . .

Pet profile

Use this section to make a list of the essential qualities of the dog you are looking for. Include all the factors you have considered in the previous chapter, from the size and coat to intelligence, trainability and cost of upkeep. Remember to keep your own profile in mind when making choices. You may find that some qualities are essential, while others are desirable. Mark your list accordingly and make sure that when it comes to being confronted by some adorable bundles of fluff at the breeder or animal shelter, you don't compromise on the qualities you have decided are right and necessary for you.

Puppy or dog . . . .

Pedigree or cross-breed . . . .

Size . . . .

Gender . . . .

Energy level . . . .

Level of exercise needed . . . .

Coat . . . .

Level of grooming required . . . .

Intelligence . . . .

Trustworthiness with children . . . .

Tolerance of other dogs . . . .

Ability to act as guard dog . . . .

Possible breeds to choose from . . . .

. . . .

. . . .

. . . .

Basic breed characteristics

The easy-to-use guide on pages 152–56 gives you some of the
basic features of all the dog breeds listed in this book to help you
narrow down your choice of the ideal breed for you. Full
information on the breeds is given in the previous chapter.
Remember that all the information about characteristics is
interrelated; for example, many dogs are listed as suitable for
families, but a large dog needing a lot of exercise will suit a
different type of family from a smaller dog needing a moderate
amount of exercise. In the same way, a dog listed as a potential
family dog indicates that it is sociable, but it may equally well be
the perfect dog for an adult household.

Key to chart

Group:	G	= Gun dog
	H	= Hound
	P	= Pastoral
	T	= Terrier
	TY	= Toy
	U	= Utility
	W	= Working
Sizes:	S	= Small
	M	= Medium
	L	= Large
	XL	= Extra large
Grooming:	🐕	= Little
	🐕🐕	= Moderate
	🐕🐕🐕	= Considerable
Exercise:	🐕	= Little
	🐕🐕	= Moderate
	🐕🐕🐕	= Considerable
Suitable	A	= Adult or show
environment:	C	= Country or working
	F	= Family

Breed	Group	Size	Grooming	Exercise	Suitable environment
Afghan hound	H	L	🐕🐕🐕	🐕🐕🐕	F
Airedale terrier	T	L	🐕🐕🐕	🐕🐕🐕	F
Basset hound	H	M	🐕	🐕🐕🐕	C / F
Beagle	H	M	🐕	🐕🐕🐕	C / F
Bedlington terrier	T	M	🐕🐕🐕	🐕🐕	F
Bernese mountain dog	W	XL	🐕🐕	🐕🐕	C / F
Bloodhound	H	L	🐕	🐕🐕🐕	C
Border collie	P	M	🐕🐕🐕	🐕🐕🐕	C / F
Border terrier	T	S	🐕🐕	🐕🐕	C / F
Borzoi	H	L	🐕🐕🐕	🐕🐕	A
Boston terrier	U	S	🐕	🐕🐕	F
Boxer	W	L	🐕	🐕🐕🐕	F
Bull terrier	T	M	🐕	🐕🐕	F
Bulldog	U	M	🐕	🐕🐕	F
Cairn terrier	T	S	🐕🐕	🐕🐕	A / F

Breed	Group	Size	Grooming	Exercise	Suitable environment
Chihuahua	TY	S	🐕	🐕	A
Chow chow	U	L	🐕🐕🐕	🐕🐕	A
Cocker spaniel	G	M	🐕🐕🐕	🐕🐕	F
Collie, rough	P	L	🐕🐕🐕	🐕🐕🐕	F
Dachshund, smooth-haired	H	M	🐕	🐕🐕	A / F
Dalmatian	U	L	🐕	🐕🐕🐕	C / F
Dandie Dinmont terrier	T	M	🐕🐕🐕	🐕🐕	A / F
Deerhound	H	L	🐕🐕	🐕🐕🐕	C
Dobermann	W	L	🐕	🐕🐕🐕	C
Elkhound	H	L	🐕🐕	🐕🐕🐕	C / F
English setter	G	L	🐕🐕🐕	🐕🐕🐕	F
English springer spaniel	G	M	🐕🐕	🐕🐕🐕	F
Field spaniel	G	M	🐕🐕🐕	🐕🐕🐕	C
Fox terrier, wire and smooth	T	M	🐕🐕🐕	🐕🐕	F

Breed	Group	Size	Grooming	Exercise	Suitable environment
Foxhound	H	L	🐕	🐕🐕🐕	C
German shepherd dog	P	L	🐕🐕	🐕🐕🐕	F
Gordon setter	G	L	🐕🐕	🐕🐕🐕	F
Great Dane	W	XL	🐕	🐕🐕🐕	C
Greyhound	H	L	🐕	🐕🐕🐕	F
Irish setter	G	L	🐕🐕🐕	🐕🐕🐕	F
Irish terrier	T	M	🐕🐕	🐕🐕	F
Irish water spaniel	G	M	🐕🐕🐕	🐕🐕🐕	C
Irish wolfhound	H	XL	🐕🐕	🐕🐕🐕	C
Jack Russell terrier	n/a	S	🐕	🐕🐕	F
Keeshound	U	M	🐕🐕🐕	🐕🐕	F
Kerry blue terrier	T	M	🐕🐕🐕	🐕🐕	F
King Charles spaniel	TY	S	🐕🐕	🐕	F / A
Lhasa apso	U	S	🐕🐕🐕	🐕	A
Manchester terrier	T	M	🐕	🐕🐕	F

Breed	Group	Size	Grooming	Exercise	Suitable environment
Mastiff	W	XL	🐕	🐕🐕	C
Miniature pinscher	TY	S	🐕	🐕	F / A
Old English sheepdog	P	L	🐕🐕🐕	🐕🐕🐕	C / F
Papillon	TY	S	🐕🐕🐕	🐕	A / F
Pekinese	TY	S	🐕🐕🐕	🐕	A
Pointer	G	L	🐕	🐕🐕🐕	F / C
Pointer, German short-haired	G	L	🐕	🐕🐕🐕	F / C
Pomeranian	TY	S	🐕🐕🐕	🐕	A
Poodle	U	L	🐕🐕🐕	🐕🐕🐕	F / A
Pug	TY	S	🐕	🐕	A
Pyrenean mountain dog	P	XL	🐕🐕🐕	🐕🐕	C
Retriever, golden	G	L	🐕🐕	🐕🐕🐕	F
Retriever, labrador	G	L	🐕	🐕🐕🐕	F
Rottweiler	W	L	🐕	🐕🐕🐕	C

Breed	Group	Size	Grooming	Exercise	Suitable environment
Saint Bernard	W	XL	🐕🐕🐕	🐕🐕	C
Saluki	H	L	🐕🐕	🐕🐕🐕	A
Samoyed	P	L	🐕🐕🐕	🐕🐕🐕	F
Schnauzer	U	M	🐕🐕🐕	🐕🐕	F
Scottish terrier	T	M	🐕🐕🐕	🐕🐕	A / F
Sealyham	T	M	🐕🐕🐕	🐕🐕	A / F
Shetland sheepdog	P	M	🐕🐕🐕	🐕🐕	F
Shih tzu	U	S	🐕🐕🐕	🐕🐕	A
Skye terrier	T	M	🐕🐕	🐕🐕	F
Weimaraner	G	L	🐕	🐕🐕🐕	F
Welsh corgi	P	M	🐕	🐕🐕	A / F
Welsh terrier	T	M	🐕🐕🐕	🐕🐕	F
West Highland white terrier	T	S	🐕🐕🐕	🐕🐕	A / F
Whippet	H	M	🐕	🐕🐕🐕	F
Yorkshire terrier	TY	S	🐕🐕🐕	🐕	A / F

Chapter 5
Buying Your Dog

O nce you have decided on your ideal dog, what should you do next? The first thing to remember is that if you really want to make the right choice you may not be able to find the perfect dog in the first place you look. Buying a dog is not like buying groceries, which you just pick off the shelf as and when you want them. This is a long-term commitment so it may take a little time and patience before you succeed. Particularly if there are children involved, make sure they realise that it is far more important to find the **right** dog than to find a dog **today**.

Wherever you go to buy your dog, you are looking for a dog or puppy that matches the profile you have set; it should also be healthy, active and have a good temperament. Its age is important in only one respect: generally speaking, a puppy should not be separated from its mother until it is eight weeks old.

Where do I buy my dog?

There are a number of options open to you when buying a dog – a breeder, an animal shelter, an advertisement in the local paper – but the common factor is that you should always buy an animal from a reputable source. Wherever you go, find out about the sellers' credentials, ask for references from satisfied customers and follow them up. Also ask at your local veterinary surgery, talk to them about your choice and ask for their advice – they have the necessary expertise to guide you in your choice. It is unwise to trust your own judgment entirely, and much better to seek the advice of people you already know and respect.

You will find that plenty of puppies are advertised in the local papers at relatively cheap prices, but you can easily buy a load of trouble by paying a very low price for a puppy. Puppies should not come cheap – think about the cost of caring for the bitch well before the birth of the puppies, plus the feed, general and veterinary care of the dam and the litter until they are ready to sell. It all adds up to a considerable amount, and the breeder has to consider this when setting the price of the puppy. If the price is very low, it could well be that something has been omitted to make it possible, and you could end up with high veterinary bills during the first year.

Breeders

A responsible breeder will be looking for a responsible owner, so they will be more than happy that you ask questions, and find out as much as you can about them and about the puppy. They should also be asking you questions to make sure their puppy is going to a good home. They'll want to know about your circumstances, your family, how you intend to train the dog, and whether you are buying the animal as a pet or to breed or show. If you are buying a puppy with a view to showing or breeding, the breeder may well discuss how they can remain involved with the puppy and give you further advice. They may even pick the most suitable puppy for you once they have found out what you are looking for.

To find a responsible breeder, go to dog shows or events, talk to owners and other breeders, contact your local breed club, or ask your local vet. Most breeders concentrate on just one breed so that they can become really expert in that type of dog. Telephone a few different breeders and talk to them before you visit. They should be happy to discuss their breeding successes, earlier customers or anything else you want to know about how they work. Remember, you are looking not only for technical expertise but also for people who are really concerned about their animals.

Ideally, I like to see animals that are raised around people in a family environment, especially if you are looking for a family pet, but some excellent breeders house their dogs in kennels. In either case, the surroundings should be well maintained and the dogs should have plenty of space. They should look happy, healthy and well cared for. Visit when the puppies are likely to be active so you can see that they are strong and vigorous.

You should be able to see the dam, but it is quite possible that you will not be able to see the sire as breeders do not always use their own stud dogs; they usually research the best dog for the bitch, and he may have been brought from some distance away. However, the breeder will have full information on him and his pedigree. Learn as much as you can about the parents to give you more idea about how the puppy is likely to turn out, and to add to your knowledge of the standards of the breed. Ask to see their pedigree registrations.

Try to choose a puppy from an average-sized litter for the breed. If the litter is too large, the puppies may not be as healthy; if it is small, they may not be as sociable. Ask how often the bitch is bred – it is not good for her to be bred every season. Check whether there were any delivery problems, or whether either the parents or the puppies have shown any signs of ill-health. If the breed tends to be subject to any specific health problems (for example, some large breeds may be prone to developing hip dysplasia), a good breeder will have the puppies screened in advance and will be able to show you the relevant veterinary certificates. All puppies should have had a veterinary check and have been given a clean bill of health. Find out whether they have been wormed and inoculated. Also ask whether the breeder will be undertaking any early training before you take the puppy home.

Many breeders will have a formal contract of sale, and it is a good idea to have everything clearly down in writing.

Some breeders have a waiting list and only breed when they have found homes for all the puppies. If this is the case, find out when puppies are likely to be available.

Pet shops

It is not generally advisable to purchase any puppy, pedigree or crossbreed, from a pet shop or dealer. If buying a pedigree dog you should try to buy direct from a specialist breeder. A pet shop or dealer may have several breeds of dog for sale and these may have been obtained from various sources so their health and condition may be difficult to determine. A breeder who specialises in one or two breeds is more likely to have detailed knowledge of the breed concerned and be able to offer advice and help where necessary.

It is also advisable to see a puppy with the dam (mother) in its home environment. You will then be able to see the conditions in which the puppy has been reared and try to learn a little about the temperament of the breeding stock. A specialist breeder may also have other dogs from similar breeding lines, so you may have the opportunity to see some of the puppy's relatives from previous litters. This can give you some idea of how the puppy might develop.

Animal shelters

If you buy from a reputable animal shelter, you are more likely to be offered an adult dog. The first thing to find out is why it is at the shelter: it may have been picked up as a stray, it may have been ill-treated, or it may have been reluctantly given up by someone too elderly or infirm to continue to care for them. Alternatively, it may have been rejected because of behavioural problems. Whatever the reason, make sure you know the implications of its history, because you must be confident that you can deal with any continuing problems.

Most animal shelters neuter the animal before it is sold to you, or you may be required to pay for it. It should have a clean bill of health from a vet, and all its inoculations should be up to date. Ask for written evidence of this.

It is a good idea to make several visits and spend some time getting to know the animals. Take them for walks if you can, watch their reaction to humans, traffic and other animals. Try to get the best possible picture of their temperament before you make your choice. Do remember, though, that you can't save them all; you must choose the one that best fits the profile you have established of the dog that will suit you and your family.

Chapter 6
Housing and Equipment

Housing a dog is not a problem, as most dogs nowadays live indoors in complete comfort, usually in the kitchen. Some larger breeds and working dogs are housed outdoors in kennels.

Dogs in the house

Undoubtedly the kitchen is the best place for your dog to live if it is kept indoors. By this I do not mean banning it completely from all other parts of the house – that can come later. But start off in the kitchen where the floor and cupboards are likely to be wipe-clean and, since there is little furniture, there is less likelihood of precious items being chewed, or knocked over by an enthusiastic wagging tail. When it is old enough, by all means let it have its share of the living-room fire; it will probably be a very generous share too, if I know anything about the average dog. Bedrooms should definitely be barred, however. Be firm and consistent from the start and teach your puppy good habits from the beginning. Stairs are easily recognisable and it will quickly understand that it must not go up them. If you let it go upstairs or sleep on your bed as a puppy, it simply will not understand when you change your mind and insist it stays downstairs and sleeps in its own bed. However, any 'disobedience' will be entirely your own fault. Far better to set down the rules on what is and what is not allowed right from the start – and stick to them.

Another point about keeping a puppy in the kitchen is that it is the best place to start training the dog to be clean. It is also a good place to begin the dog's training to be alert to callers. Encourage it to announce their arrival by barking even at an early age, but also teach the dog to understand the meaning of the word 'Quiet!'

The outdoors dog

A dog that lives outside need be no less happy than a house dog as long as it has the right accommodation. Generally speaking, the dog should be at least four months old before it is expected to live outside on its own and even then preferably with the company of other dogs.

A dry, roomy kennel with an adjoining run is probably the ideal accommodation. You could make your own kennel, or you may have a suitable shed, garage or outbuilding. It must have good ventilation, keep the dog warm, dry and comfortable, and be able to be locked at night. The dog can have a bed and blanket, or some people use shredded paper for bedding, as this can be changed daily and destroyed. The dog must also have a large, secure run if it is not free to roam the garden or house during the day.

Beds

My favoured style for a dog's bed is a small wooden or plastic box, raised slightly off the ground to avoid draughts. Many people prefer the idea of a basket, but these are full of nooks and crannies that can trap dirt and germs, while a smooth plastic or wooden bed can more easily be scrubbed regularly. Line the bed with a soft blanket or piece of nylon fur fabric, which will be comfortable to lie on and easy to wash. Shake out the blanket every morning and leave it to air in the open when not in use. Place the bed in a draught-free corner; you might be surprised how draughty it is in your kitchen at ground level, so try lying on the floor yourself before you site the bed to make sure it is not in an unpleasantly cold spot. It also needs to be placed somewhere out of the way so no one trips over it.

Essential equipment

Apart from the dog's bed, there is very little equipment that is necessary to keep your dog happy.

Drinking and feeding dishes

The puppy must have its own drinking and feeding dishes, which can be plastic, metal or earthenware. They should be easy to clean, and with no corners where stale food could lurk. There are all sorts of shapes and sizes, so be careful to choose one suitable for your dog. For example, if you have a spaniel, you can buy a special bowl that is small at the top, allowing just enough space for the dog's mouth but ensuring that its ears hang outside. All dogs must have fresh water available at all times, and this should be placed by the dog's bed. Look for the type of dish that cannot be knocked over easily and avoid any that can be gripped in the dog's teeth and turned over.

Grooming equipment

You will not need to use a brush and comb much on a very young puppy, but you should get the puppy used to being groomed regularly from three or four months old. The average family dog gets nothing like enough grooming – five minutes every day is much less time and trouble in the long run than lengthy sessions at more irregular intervals. The comb should be made of steel, with or without a handle as you prefer, and the teeth set coarse or fine according to the nature of the dog's coat. Dog brushes are also very varied. A dog with a short coat will need a hard, short bristle. A longer, silky coat will call for a handle brush with wire bristles set in a rubber pad; this type is very thorough in its work and does not tear the coat in any way, and it is easy to clear of loose hair. It is a good idea to get information on suitable grooming kit from the breeder of the puppy or from your nearest pet shop.

If you are going to bath your dog, you'll need a suitable pet shampoo and conditioner. You can also buy spray-on pet conditioner to use when grooming a dry coat.

If you need to cut the dog's toenails, you should buy special clippers. Dogs that are walked regularly out of doors should not need this, however, as their nails will wear down naturally.

Some dogs, such as poodles, require regular clipping to keep their coat clean and tidy. This can be done by a professional groomer, who will also bath the dog, cut its toenails and clean its ears.

A few breeds, such as cocker spaniels and West Highland terriers, require regular stripping, which means having their coat thinned. Unless you are experienced at dog grooming, do not try to use a stripping knife yourself. It is best done by a professional dog groomer.

Collar and lead

When the puppy first arrives, it is not a good idea to take it into the street (unless you have a garden to exercise it in). It is only a baby, whatever breed it is, and will not run very far at this stage. A very young puppy loves company and you may rest assured it will not wander very far from you or other human society. At about three months old, you will need to buy a collar. Choose one made of leather or nylon, as light as possible in weight so as not to bother the dog too much, and a matching lead. Alternatively, for the first collar and lead, you can buy a slip-lead, which is a one-piece lead and collar. Very cheap items are often a poor investment and can break if they get very wet but, on the other hand, don't spend a great deal on the puppy's first collar as it will outgrow it after three or four months. Buy reasonable-quality items, and take advice from the pet shop if you are not sure.

Coats

Bearing in mind that a dog is quite a hardy animal, I do not recommend the regular use of a coat, although there are exceptional cases, such as convalescence, continual wet weather and so on. There are coats for warmth and coats for protection from rain, and these can be useful to prevent the need for excessive drying and grooming of some breeds in bad weather. If you do use a dog coat, make quite sure it fits well, particularly underneath and over the chest of the dog.

Toys

Puppies are playful and inquisitive creatures and will love a few items to play with. Toys can help to settle the puppy into its new surroundings, and give it something to occupy its time and distract its attention from the fact that it is no longer with the rest of the litter. It can be a rubber bone, an old slipper, or one of the many rubber or hard nylon toys you can buy from a pet shop. You can tie the object to the dog's bed by a length of cord. A puppy will usually be more interested in the cord than the toy, but this does not matter very much as long as it keeps the dog occupied. If a puppy is bored, it may well start to chew on its bed, or anything else it can find, and you should not allow this. A puppy will soon learn that its own toys are for chewing and your belongings and furniture (of any kind) are not – but only if, as with everything, you are firm and consistent.

Chapter 7
Feeding

A dog's digestive process is similar to our own (although much more robust), so dogs need food for growth, energy and protection in the same way that we do. You need to provide your dog with a healthy balanced diet that fulfils all these needs, and is appropriate to its age and breed. Fortunately for us, a dog can exist on all sorts of food, but feeding a poor diet over a prolonged period will be just as bad for its health as it would for ours, so get into good habits from the start and your dog will remain fit and healthy.

Feeding your puppy

Puppies spend the first two months of their life with their mother. A tiny puppy will certainly require nothing more than its mother's milk to feed it for the first three to four weeks and, providing she is well cared for and gets ample nourishment, the puppy will have all it needs. It will hardly see the world at this stage and will just eat and sleep with the rest of the litter.

At three to six weeks, depending on its development, the puppy will start to be fed on tiny quantities of a good-quality puppy food. The puppy will advance day by day until at two months it will be quite able to leave its mother and live independently. This is when puppies are usually separated from their mother and go to their new homes – which means you take over their care. Make sure you have discussed appropriate feeding with the breeder or whoever sells you the puppy, so you know what to do. Find out what the puppy is used to, and what quantities and consistency of food to start with. Most breeders will provide you with a diet sheet.

At this age, the puppy will need very careful feeding at three-hourly intervals during the day (four or five feeds a day), the food being given with gradually less water as the puppy becomes accustomed to chewing. Although quantities are important, it is impossible to lay down hard and fast rules, and probably the best guide is the puppy's development. It is certainly safer to underfeed than to give too much. The size and breed of the dog will make a difference, of course, but if you use a good-quality food, you can't go far wrong. The last meal of the day should be given early enough before 'bedtime' for the dog to go out into the garden to start house-training.

The average puppy in good health will bolt its food readily and would seem to have an endless capacity, but do not give second helpings. If by any chance the puppy is not eager for food, take it away until the next mealtime. Do not leave cold or stale food lying about for the puppy to eat when it feels like it.

At 16 weeks, depending on the development of the puppy, you can probably reduce to three meals a day, and also begin to introduce hard biscuits to help in the replacement of the dog's baby teeth. At six months, reduce to two meals a day and keep to this. One meal a day is not advisable.

A healthy balanced diet

An adult dog needs a good balanced diet. Growth depends on protein, and for a dog this means that meat should normally form a large part of the diet. Energy is derived from carbohydrates and fats, while extra nutrition is given by vitamins and minerals, which are the invisible necessities of any good diet.

To provide your dog with all these elements, you have to decide how best to feed it. It is important that the diet is not too monotonous, and it is therefore a good idea to vary the food a little every now and then.

Many people now choose to feed a complete dog food that contains all the necessary elements for a healthy diet, and these come in many forms. Choose a good-quality product from your pet store, or ask your vet or breeder to recommend one if you are not sure which will be suitable.

If you are not using a complete food, you'll need to supply a range of foods. Meat can be offered as canned food or cooked meat. For carbohydrate, a wide range of dog biscuits is readily available, or you can crumble some dry, stale wholemeal bread into the dog's meal. Vitamins and minerals will be found in vegetables or household scraps, and in canned dog food.

How much to feed

This depends on the breed, age and activity level of the dog, so be guided by the information provided on the label of the feed you give, or by the breeder. You can also judge by the general condition, weight and amount of exercise of the dog to make a sensible judgment. As a very rough guide, small dogs should have 225–350 g (8–12 oz) of food a day; medium dogs need 450–750 g (1–1¾ lb); and large dogs need 900 g–1.5 kg (2–3 lb). Train yourself to keep an eye on the amount of food you give and on the dog's weight, to avoid problems that will arise as a result of over-feeding.

Something to chew

A dog should have something to chew on occasionally, such as a hard biscuit or a rubber bone, as this is good for the teeth and jaws. Some bones can be dangerous because if they splinter they can damage the dog internally. Never give cooked bones, or rabbit or chicken bones. The best source of large, uncooked bones is probably your local butcher.

If your dog picks up and chews stones, it is probably because it needs a bone or a toy to chew. Don't let this become a habit, as the stones can damage its teeth, or be swallowed and require an operation to remove them.

When to feed

Once a dog has settled into a routine of two meals a day, stick to the same time for the meals. Don't feed a dog before or immediately after exercise. I usually feed my dogs in the morning, then late in the afternoon when any strenuous exercise for the day is finished, but this will depend on the dog's routine and your own. It is a good idea to allow time for a short run after the meal has been digested.

As with a puppy, do not leave food down if the dog does not eat its meal. Take it up within ten minutes and do not feed the dog until the next mealtime. This may sound rather harsh, but the dog will soon become used to it. If the dog leaves all food untouched for more than a day or so, you may want to seek the advice of your vet. Dogs can go off their food for a variety of minor reasons – lack of exercise, hot weather, being unsettled by something in their surroundings – but it is worth isolating the cause so that you can take any necessary preventive action.

Always make sure the dog has a bowl of clean, fresh water available and change it at least once a day.

Chapter 8
Training and Routine

It is absolutely essential that you train your dog properly. This is not a book about training, but this chapter will give you an idea of what to expect.

All dogs have to be taught to behave – it does not come naturally. The dog is, after all, a creature of instinct and will automatically do whatever is necessary to satisfy its own appetites and desires. If you don't teach it to walk calmly beside you, it will bolt down the road at the sight of every other dog. It will steal food off the kitchen table – unless you have taught it to eat only things that are put in its bowl. And of course, a puppy will not understand that it must not soil the kitchen floor unless you teach it that its toilet facilities are outside only.

Training your puppy is very similar to training a young child. The key points are consistency and clarity and the earlier you start, the better. Be absolutely firm on what is and is not allowed and don't vary from that. Supervise the puppy closely; interrupt or stop it when it does something it is not allowed to do, and praise it when it is good. (Don't overdo the praise, however, or the puppy will be so distracted by being showered with affection, it will forget how it earned the praise in the first place!)

Early training

Puppy training is really all about instilling good habits and it is never too soon to start. From the day it arrives, the puppy should always sleep in its own bed, and you should keep it in the kitchen for the first few weeks or at least until it is fully toilet-trained. Once you are sure it won't have accidents, it can be introduced to the rest of the house, but don't allow it to go upstairs. The puppy will quickly understand that the stairs are a no-go zone. As I said earlier, it is no good allowing the puppy to sleep on the beds and then expecting it to understand why you change your mind when it grows up into something rather less cuddly. In the same way, don't let it sleep on the sofa if you are not prepared for that to be a habit throughout its life.

Playing games

Puppies are playful little animals and you'll get a great deal of pleasure from playing with yours. Playing is also part of their learning process, and they will not differentiate between the two in the same way that you do, so you can use the opportunity to underline your house rules. The puppy should have its own toys, and these should be the only things it is allowed to play with. If you use the hearthrug or a cushion to play tug-of-war with the puppy, its tiny mouth probably won't do much harm. But as it becomes an adult, it will continue the game with every other loose rug or blanket it finds and the damage may be considerable.

Confine boisterous games to the garden. If you do not do this, the puppy will not understand why you won't throw its rubber bone down the hall or why you should object when it tears around the room while you are watching TV.

Toilet training

Toilet training should also be started as soon as you get the puppy home. Try to feed and exercise the puppy at the same times every day, and this will help to establish the puppy's toilet routine. Create a schedule that is practical for you to keep up – if you can't adhere to a timetable, it will be unreasonable to expect the puppy to do so. Let it out of doors at frequent intervals, and always after meals and every time it wakes up from a nap. It should also go out last thing at night and first thing in the morning, giving it plenty of opportunity to go to the toilet. Most puppies will prefer to go to the toilet outside anyway, so if it makes a mistake it is generally your fault and the puppy should not be reprimanded. Don't forget that it is only a small animal and has a small bladder. Any sort of extra excitement can lead to accidents, so be prepared for a puddle if the puppy is nervous, has a sudden bad scare or gets worked up during a particularly wild play session.

It may seem a good idea to provide newspaper on the floor of the kitchen, but if you do this, the puppy may assume that it can take advantage of this facility and will get used to it, rather than learning that it is expected to perform outdoors.

Regular habits and abundant praise are the keys to success, although you may need to add quite a lot of patience and observation. Keep an eye on the puppy and if it stops playing and starts looking around for a convenient place to perform, take it outside quickly. (It may just be exploring, but you will soon learn how to know the difference!) Keep it close to you and if it has to be left alone for any length of time, confine it to an area where mess won't matter too much.

If the puppy starts to make a mess on the floor, clap your hands to draw attention to what it is doing. Whisk it outside to finish, if possible. Once it has relieved itself, bring it back and show it the mess, then, with the puppy watching, scoop the mess up and take it outside to the designated toilet area.

Obedience training

All dogs should be trained to be obedient and well behaved, and training them is something that is well within the scope of all dog owners. I think any dog should be a companion you can be proud of, should come instantly to your call, walk correctly at heel both on and off the lead, and sit or lie flat on command. There are no great secrets to success, but I cannot stress enough that you must be consistent. As with toilet training, it's a good idea to start early – and start as you mean to go on.

Start by praising everything the puppy does right. At the same time, make sure you are keeping it in a routine, with a regular sleeping place, showing it the places it is allowed to go, and so on. All these things are crucial to establishing the foundation for training: trust, respect, affection, and the knowledge that you are in charge. Winning the confidence of the puppy is crucial. Gentle encouragement for 15 minutes with a kind word is worth more than a week of strict treatment. It is not necessary to employ the use of titbits in training – I prefer to use lots of praise and most puppies are delighted simply to know that they have pleased you.

Use the puppy's name whenever you speak to it – it will learn to recognise the sound of its name very quickly. Later it will learn to respond immediately to other words, such as 'Sit' and 'Down' but you should not expect it to respond to these commands until it is several months old and you start more formal training.

The puppy should not be discouraged from barking when the doorbell rings, for example, or if it hears an unusual noise outside, but start to train him immediately to know the word 'Quiet!' and respond to your command. Say 'Quiet!' firmly (there's no need to shout). It will soon understand what you mean.

By about three months, the puppy is ready to start obedience training. Party tricks and advanced training are not necessary, although the average dog has a high intelligence and is quite capable of responding to additional training. This, however, will be based on the trust and obedience you have established with basic training, so concentrate on that first and develop 'tricks' later on. One dog I knew would walk round the kitchen with his dish in his mouth at his regular feeding time, as a gentle reminder that he was hungry! Other dogs fetch their leads as soon as you bring out the wellington boots or the shopping bag. There's plenty of scope with such an intelligent animal.

It is best if one person is responsible for the dog's daily care and training, but all members of the household – and visitors – must help to ensure that the established routine is followed quite strictly, especially at first. This makes it much easier for the dog to get into good habits and respond to what is expected of it. It is true to say that no two puppies are identical in character and temperament any more than two children are: one may have a natural aptitude for learning the difference between right and wrong, and another will be obstinate, highly strung or strong-willed.

Walking on a lead

Once a puppy has had its full course of vaccinations, you can begin to take it out and about. Don't choose an open space or park for the first few outings – it's better to stick to something like a narrow footpath, well screened on each side, naturally confining the puppy to a position behind you. If the puppy is quite young, do not introduce the lead at all, but just encourage it to follow your direction, which it will probably do quite readily providing there are no distractions. Some experienced trainers do not believe in the use of a lead at all, but I believe you must be guided by circumstances. If you are near a crowded shopping area, live on a main road or there is any danger that the puppy could run off, you must obviously use a lead.

It is a good idea to keep the lead on view before you need it, so that your puppy can see it and smell it. Hang it in its place in the kitchen, and try it on the puppy a few times before you go out so that it can get used to the idea. For small puppies you can use a light collar and lead or a harness.

The first few outings on the lead will undoubtedly try your patience more than a little, and you may have to be content simply because the puppy makes an effort to walk at all. The puppy may stand still for quite a long time, but continually dragging at the lead is useless. Patience is essential. To encourage the puppy to walk, hold a small rubber bone or ball in front of it to distract its attention from the lead. Another quite effective method of getting a puppy to walk steadily is to take a neighbour's or friend's dog out with you at the same time to walk in front of you, and thus provide a constant interest for the puppy. You have the consolation of knowing that the average puppy is very quick to learn, and after a few days you will see a great improvement. Meanwhile, train yourself to hold the lead in your left hand and give the puppy plenty of encouragement and praise when it is doing the right thing. Praising the dog will ensure that it understands that it has done the right thing, and it is essential throughout positive and happy training.

By about four months old, the puppy should walk happily on a lead and you can move on to perfecting its correct position, with its nose very close to your left leg. When the puppy has been walking for a few metres correctly at heel and on a slack lead, you should praise it and give it a few pats of encouragement. These little attentions convey a tremendous amount to the dog.

Half an hour is quite long enough for each training session. Once the puppy gets bored, you are both wasting your time.

Letting the dog off the lead

A considerable problem for many dog owners is establishing when it is safe to let the dog off the lead for the first time. I am afraid there is no hard-and-fast rule about this, but I suggest that you first make sure that the dog will walk properly to heel on a lead. Then you can try letting the dog go, with the lead still on. Let the lead drop to the ground at your side, making no unusual movement in doing so and, above all, not altering your stride in any way. The dog should carry on walking beside you as though nothing has happened. If it should try to bolt away, grab the lead quickly to stop it, saying its name firmly as you do so. The dog will soon learn that it is expected to walk beside you. I have found this practice very effective if carried out correctly and repeated a few times. You can then feel much more confident about allowing the dog off the lead. On no account forget the all-important praise during this training.

I cannot stress strongly enough that no dog should ever be left off the lead when near a road, however obedient or well trained. It is totally unfair on both the dog and the car drivers and is simply not worth the risk of the heartache that can be caused if the dog does run into the road. For the same reason, you should not allow the dog to run freely round the park while you stand and chat, play with the children on the swings, etc. You should keep your eye on it all the time.

Learning to sit and lie down

When the puppy is approaching six months of age, you can start the next step, which is to learn to sit and lie on command. These, of course, are two quite separate movements and require two different words of command. The words 'Sit' and 'Down' are the best ones to use, as both are short and lend themselves to emphatic pronunciation. Always use the same word of command for the same movement, and only repeat the order once in a slightly raised voice.

To start with, you will need to place the dog in the sitting or lying position while simultaneously repeating the word 'Sit' or 'Down'. As soon as the dog shows some signs of understanding what you want, stop handling the dog and use the word of command only. Don't say anything but the actual word of command during the lesson time. If the dog fails to obey either on command or on the first repetition, then go back to the beginning again by placing it in the required position and repeating the word. If you fail to do this, the puppy will probably assume that it can take its time to obey, and will need to be spoken to six or seven times before obeying.

Once you have established this, practise the command while you are out walking. Stop abruptly, and immediately the dog stops, give the command 'Sit' or 'Down', as the case may be. Give the dog a chance to correct a wrong move, and remember to give praise when the puppy gets it right.

Punishment

Training should be a positive and happy experience for both you and the dog, and it is absolutely essential to keep praising the animal when it gets things right. Most problems arise when we fail to use our own intelligence and forget that a dog cannot understand what we say unless we teach it first, or that it doesn't understand if we keep changing our minds.

A dog should never be punished for a mistake and especially not for a mistake that is your fault. If the dog is wilfully disobedient, a sharp word at the time and place will let it know that it cannot get away with it. Never scold a dog after the event; it will have no idea what it is being punished for, will lose trust and become scared, and will be very difficult to train at all. 'Wait till your father gets home' never worked for either a dog or a child!

Training an adult dog

The old saying, 'You can't teach an old dog new tricks' is simply not true. Certainly, if you adopt an adult dog, it may already have habits that you want to change through training, but dogs are intelligent and mature animals so are quite capable of being retrained, even though it may be a little more difficult than training a puppy from the start.

The principles are exactly the same as those outlined above for training a puppy: establish trust, confidence and respect for authority; stick to a routine; be totally consistent; give constant reassurance and praise.

Training a dog to interact with other animals

The dog is by nature a friendly animal and, although it is the principle pet in the average home, it is not usually opposed to a little company other than human.

Many thousands of homes keep both a cat and a dog, and they are nearly always the best of friends, in spite of the fact that the cat is supposed to be the dog's natural enemy. If you buy a puppy and a kitten together, then they will grow up being quite used to each other. However, if you are introducing a dog into a home where the cat is firmly established, you will simply need to train them to get used to each other. All the principles you have established in terms of good training apply here as well. Establish the rules and stick to them.

To start with, place the dog in its own room so that the existing pet can smell it but not see it. Then move the dog to another room and allow the original pet to explore the room where it has been kept. You can then introduce the animals to each other, making sure you keep a close eye on them and react quickly if their instincts are aggressive.

See that all the family makes a great fuss of the old-established pet while it is getting used to the new one, to relieve its natural feelings of jealousy. Move slowly and patiently and don't try to rush things.

Training dogs and children

Children and dogs do go together. In fact, any animal can be the source of a great deal of education to a child, to say nothing of the companionship that can be established between them. There are, of course, reported instances of dogs injuring children, but no dog will normally make an unprovoked attack on a child without good reason and these instances are usually related to bad training and lack of control.

I think it is true to say, however, that babies or toddlers and puppies don't mix. With the best possible intentions, a two-year-old may pull a puppy's ears or tail or poke its eye while trying to be friendly, while a puppy may scratch or knock over a toddler while playing. If you already have a dog and then a baby comes along, you will need to be very strict in keeping them both under supervision until they are old enough to interact safely.

Once a child is four or five years of age and has both more physical control and more understanding of the difference between right and wrong, then is the time to have the puppy. The two youngsters will grow up together and develop a thorough mutual understanding.

Children should be taught from an early age that they should never touch a strange dog. If the owner is with the dog and gives permission, then it is up to you, the parent, to decide whether or not you will allow your child to pet the dog.

Fitting into your routine

I have already talked about establishing a routine for your dog, and this is very important. Like us, dogs are creatures of habit, so most dogs are quite happy to fit into the daily routine of the household. It is amazing how quickly a dog will get used to your daily routine and begin to fit into it. It will soon learn that when you reach for your coat that means an outing, and many dogs will fetch their own leads off the coat rack on a given cue. You can combine the dog's walk with a trip to the shops or a walk to a friend's house, thereby killing two birds with one stone.

The important thing is that the routine should suit both you and the dog, so if you go out jogging at a certain time each day and plan your meals accordingly, you can also plan the dog's meals to coincide.

Exercise

There are many conflicting opinions about exercise and how much is necessary for the dog's well-being, but it is impossible to lay down hard-and-fast rules. The breed of the dog is very important, of course. A German shepherd's needs cannot be compared with those of a dachshund, for example. Personally, I think it is a little hard on any dog to be confined to the garden all the time – even if it belongs to one of the smaller breeds. Dogs should be walked regularly and given a chance to run off the lead in a suitable park or in open country, although obviously the larger and more energetic dogs will run further and faster than the smaller ones.

First thing in the morning and in the late afternoon are good times to exercise a dog, and do make sure that energetic runs are not too close to mealtimes.

Chapter 9
Keeping Dogs Healthy

A healthy dog is a happy dog. The average dog should not suffer from many illnesses. If it is healthy to begin with and has been fed, exercised and cared for in a sensible way, it should lead a happy and healthy life to an average age of 12 to 14 years, depending on the breed.

Dogs are very quick to show if they are off-colour, and though they cannot explain what is wrong or how they feel, there are usually certain unmistakable symptoms that the watchful owner can detect. If this is the case, you should immediately take action to sort out the problem and seek the appropriate advice and treatment as necessary.

Grooming

Regular grooming is part of maintaining a dog's health and well-being. It will keep the dog's coat in good condition, and obviously is particularly important with long-haired breeds. Although you can send your dog to a professional dog groomer, much of the regular care can – and should – be done by you. Choose a convenient time of day, perhaps after the morning walk, for grooming, which should take only about ten minutes if it is done regularly. If it is wet outside, the dog should always be rubbed down with a towel when it returns to the house – especially for long-haired breeds – so keep an old but clean dog towel handy. Don't attempt to comb a dog's coat when it is wet. Once it is dry, give the dog a thorough brush or comb, depending on what is best for its type of coat. Some coats may benefit from a conditioning spray before you groom. The dog will soon become used to being groomed and will stand still and enjoy the process. If you don't give your dog regular grooming, it will be restless when you do and you will both find it a chore.

There are a few other regular checks you should make, perhaps once a week. Check the dog's ears to make sure there is no build-up of wax, and make sure its anus and eyes are clean. If it walks regularly on hard surfaces, its toenails should wear down naturally; otherwise you may need to clip them occasionally. If you do, make sure you do not clip the quick (the coloured part at the base of the nail) or it will bleed; if you are in any doubt, ask an expert to show you.

Similarly, it is a good idea to give your dog an occasional bath, so that it gets used to it and won't make a fuss when it becomes necessary. Most short-coated dogs don't require frequent baths, but long-haired varieties may need regular bathing to stop their coats becoming matted. Make sure the water is just warmer than body temperature and that the dog has a non-slip mat to stand on. Use an appropriate dog shampoo, stroking it in gently rather than rubbing, and rinse it out thoroughly. You may also like to use a dog conditioner, then rinse again very thoroughly.

Towel-dry the coat gently, then let the dog have a good shake. You can use a hairdryer on a warm setting if you wish, gently brushing the coat as it becomes drier. Don't let the dog get cold.

For rough-coated breeds, it is a good idea to keep the coat short to make it more manageable. It will need trimming at least twice during the summer. Breeds such as the cocker spaniel should be kept trimmed around the feet, leg feathers and ears. Some dogs have coats that need regular professional stripping. Ask your vet or breeder for recommendations for local dog groomers before you choose where to take your dog for attention.

As a general rule, dogs should not need a coat conditioner on a regular basis, provided they are getting a good-quality balanced diet and plenty of exercise. If you are concerned about the condition of your dog's coat, you should talk to your vet.

Worming

Nearly all puppies between eight and 16 weeks will need worming to get rid of intestinal parasites, if this has not already been done by the breeder. There is always a possibility that you will need to do it a second time. The most effective preparations are only available from your veterinary surgeon, so you are advised to buy from them rather than buying from a pet shop.

There are a number of symptoms that clearly indicate when your puppy is suffering from worms. There may be actual worms in the droppings, the puppy may have an unpleasant habit of scratching its anus, or it may show a clear indication, such as looking very pinched at the loins or suffering a bout of diarrhoea. If you are in any way uncertain, talk to the breeder or to your vet.

Adult dogs should be treated for worms every six months to ensure that they never suffer from these intestinal problems.

Inoculations

All puppies should be given a full course of inoculations, starting at between eight and 12 weeks, to protect them from parvovirus, leptospirosis, distemper and hepatitis. Vaccination is the only method of protection from these serious diseases, which have either no cure or, in the case of leptospirosis, no reliable cure. The breeder may already have started the inoculations when you get the puppy but it is up to you to complete the course.

Regular boosters are also essential, as protection is not lifelong and pets are at risk if they come into contact with the diseases without up-to-date vaccinations. Ask your vet about all the injections that will be necessary for your puppy when you take it for its first check-up.

If your dog is to go into kennels, you will be expected to produce a certificate showing that all its inoculations are up to date.

Neutering

You are responsible for all aspects of your dog's health and welfare, and this includes whether or not you want them to breed. Unless you specifically want to breed from your pet, you should speak to your vet about getting the animal neutered. If you decide not to neuter your pet for any reason, you may find that you have problems with control and discipline. Bitches that are not neutered must be kept away from other dogs when on heat and you will need to be prepared to keep your unneutered dog under control if it smells a bitch on heat. Many dogs will also show an increased desire to wander if they are not neutered, even when there is not a bitch on heat in the vicinity.

If you are going to breed the animals, check with your vet that the dog or bitch is healthy and suitable for breeding, and look into the details in advance by talking with experts and reading up on the subject.

Prevention of disease

Dogs are hardy animals, but this does not mean that we can neglect certain precautions in their care and maintenance, especially with regard to a few particularly virulent diseases that are common only to them. Good-quality regular food and exercise are, of course, the best places to start. An overweight or unfit dog is more prone to problems, especially of the respiratory system.

Cleanliness is all-important, not only of the dog itself but also its bedding and its feeding bowls. It is astonishing how many problems can start from this source, and you cannot take too much trouble. You may always clean the feeding bowl after each meal, but how many of us take the trouble to clean a collar and lead once in a while or scrub out the dog's bed or basket several times during the year? It is certainly something that should be part of your routine.

Inevitably, a certain amount of trouble can be picked up on the streets, and I think it is a good idea for young puppies to remain within their own domain until they are at least a few months old or until after they have been inoculated. It is certainly a case of 'better safe than sorry'. Diseases can also spread from areas where numerous dogs congregate, so if you are in any doubt, avoid such places in parks or streets. If you know that someone has been in contact with an unwell animal, don't let them fondle your dog. It goes without saying that any animal suspected of having contracted a disease should always be isolated.

As with human ailments, many serious complaints start from getting too cold, and a dog that has been out in the wet should be rubbed down when you get home. Make sure the dog is not allowed to sleep in a draught, especially in cold or wet weather. This applies particularly to domestic dogs, which may not be quite as resilient as the sporting varieties that enjoy the freedom of the country all day.

Dealing with common illnesses

Colds

The usual symptoms of a cold are shivering and some slight discharge from the eyes and nose; the appetite may not be affected in the early stages. Treatment is very simple: keep the dog warm and comfortable. Do not give it cold food for a few days – warm it just so that the chill is taken off.

If a cold is neglected, it is possible that it can lead to bronchitis, which is obviously much more serious, particularly if the animal is older. In this case, a cough or choking sound is present, and possibly a wheeziness, particularly when asleep. Simple treatment is again the best. Keep the dog in a warm room and at a constant temperature; a small dog might benefit from a warm coat that covers the chest and stomach. A sick dog must not be allowed to get wet or chilled, so suspend long walks if the weather is miserable. An overweight dog is more likely to have health problems and will make the worst patient, so avoid the problem of excess weight by sensible feeding and if it occurs, reduce it by dieting.

If you are in any doubt about what to do, or if the dog's condition does not improve, contact your vet straight away.

Constipation and diarrhoea

Constipation is one of the most common of all the minor ailments, and will show by the dog straining excessively. It is usually a sign of the wrong food or not enough exercise.

Immediately you notice the problem, give the dog a mild laxative in the form of liquid paraffin, or in the case of young dogs and puppies 5 ml/1 tsp warm salad oil. From my experience, I have not found caster oil satisfactory. Since you don't want the problem to recur, check your that you are feeding the dog a good balanced diet and that it is getting enough exercise.

Diarrhoea, particularly in puppies, should be viewed with more concern as it can be the forerunner of something more serious and must therefore be treated immediately. One of the most common causes is the wrong food, either the wrong puppy mixture or food for adult dogs that is a bit 'high'. Put the dog on a light diet and make sure the food is warm and the problem should resolve itself. If it doesn't clear within 48 hours or is particularly severe, contact your vet. Make sure that the problem does not recur by checking the dog's regular diet.

Gastroenteritis can follow the symptoms of diarrhoea, particularly in young dogs, and must always be treated by a vet. This is an inflammation of the intestines and may be caused by a chill or incorrect diet. You can identify the condition by the fact that the dog passes a thin and greenish excreta, will strain considerably and suffer some pain. The dog will not necessarily appear listless, but may have no interest in food of any kind. In general, 24 hours of fasting followed by a light diet of puppy food should solve the problem, but, as I have said, you should be advised by your vet.

Skin problems

Skin problems that can affect dogs commonly come under the headings of eczema and mange. Though external complaints, they are promoted to a great extent by internal disorders, but are usually fairly easily dealt with.

Eczema is set up by a condition of the blood caused by bad feeding, inadequate food or internal parasites. It is not contagious. Make sure everything is kept scrupulously clean and seek advice on treatment from your vet.

Mange is caused by mites and shows itself as red patches on the skin and hair loss. There are two main types, sarcoptic and follicular, and you should seek advice on treatment from your vet.

Other problems

Parvovirus is another serious problem that shows similar symptoms to gastroenteritis and is almost always fatal. You should have your puppy vaccinated against this when it is about 12 weeks old (see page 193).

Another serious condition from which a dog can suffer is distemper, although this is now extremely uncommon due to the regular administration of vaccines, and all responsible dog owners should have their pets vaccinated. This is also true of leptospirosis.

Choosing a vet

Finding a good vet is important. It is a good idea to register with a local veterinary practice before you even buy your dog, and obviously you will be visiting them to have your puppy vaccinated.

Ask for recommendations from friends or local breeders, or go through the local telephone directory or Yellow Pages; then telephone or visit the surgeries before you make your choice. Choose a practice that is easily accessible from your home; you don't want to be travelling miles just for a routine jab or when your dog is ill.

You are looking for a well-qualified and highly reputable veterinary practice where you feel comfortable that your dog is going to receive the best of care. Go to the surgery and look at the facilities; check that the surgery is clean and well appointed; ask about the surgery hours and the number of vets in the practice; find out about emergency cover; ask about their basic costs. Try to visit in surgery hours so you can see that the animals in their care are happy and that they are well treated, and that the staff are friendly and knowledgeable.

If you have a pedigree dog, there may be a local vet who specialises in that breed and this can be useful since some breeds can be prone to specific health problems.

Pet insurance

It is a good idea to take out pet insurance for your dog. Policies vary, but you can obtain cover for vets' fees for consultation and medication in case of illness, kennel costs if you become ill yourself, compensation for the loss or death of your pet, holiday cover and third party insurance. This last is very important – if your dog causes a road traffic accident or damages someone else's property, you could be liable for a considerable amount of money. Costs vary, so you should shop around as you would for any kind of insurance, but are likely to be in the region of £200 annually. There will be an excess, and the cost of injections is not normally covered.

Your local veterinary surgery will have details of some insurance plans. You can also obtain information from the RSPCA.

Chapter 10
Travelling

The average dog is usually quite happy travelling – and is often less trouble than a young child! If it is with its owner, it will feel quite confident and settle down happily for the journey.

In the car

A dog will probably take more kindly to car travel if it has been introduced to it as a puppy and has become used to it. Start by allowing the dog to sit in the stationery car, so it gets used to the surroundings and the smell. Then start with short journeys and, as with all dog training, be firm and consistent.

The dog should always travel in the back seat or in the luggage section. Don't forget that the back of the car can become very warm, especially if there is luggage packed in the dog's travelling space. Never allow your dog to sit in the front, even on another passenger's lap. If it becomes excited for any reason, it may distract or jump on the driver, and if the car stops suddenly, it will be thrown through the windscreen. Put down a rug or blanket for the dog to lie on and make sure the dog is restrained by its lead or a purpose-made dog harness. It should have enough freedom of movement to be comfortable but not so much so that it could move too freely around the car and disturb the driver, or climb out of the car at any time.

If you need to leave the dog in the car, it should be quite content to sit in a comfortable seat on guard while you are away. However, you must make sure that you park the car in the shade and provide plenty of fresh air by leaving a window slightly open. Don't forget that the sun will move round while you are away, so check that the car will not be in full sun by the time you come back. Remember that the car will heat up very quickly when stationary, so you must be absolutely sure that the dog will remain comfortable while you are gone.

Public transport

Before you embark on a journey on public transport of any kind, make sure there are no restrictions on travelling with a dog. A well-behaved dog is not usually forbidden, but it is at the discretion of the guard or conductor, and it is unreasonable to take a large dog on a crowded bus, for example. You may have to travel on the top deck of a double-decker bus, so make sure your dog is able – and willing – to climb the stairs. You may also be expected to pay the child's fare for the dog.

If your dog is well trained, you should have no trouble taking it on public transport, but do think not only about the dog's well-being but also that of the other passengers. There is nothing more annoying than a dog in a train or on a bus making a nuisance of itself by jumping over everyone and climbing on the seats. This is quite unnecessary and gives a bad name to other people travelling with pets. Always keep the dog on a lead and under control.

If the dog is nervous of trains or buses, pick it up to board or alight from the vehicle. There is no good purpose to be served by insisting that a nervous animal should board the vehicle itself. Minimise the dog's fear of the unusual by carrying it firmly on to the train or bus and give it plenty of reassurance.

Motion sickness

Never feed a dog before a journey. If it is a long journey, you can give some food on the way once the animal has become accustomed to the experience of travelling. If you think your dog may be ill during an unavoidable journey, sit the dog on an old raincoat or a specially designed seat protector so you do not have to worry too much if the worst happens. If you are anxious yourself, that will transmit to the dog.

If your dog does suffer seriously from motion sickness, especially in cars, you can seek your vet's advice on a preventive medicine to help your animal through the journey, although it is better if you can travel by another means.

International travel

If you are travelling internationally with a dog, there are strict rules governing health and safety, and some formalities required both by the government and shipping or airline companies.

Contact your travel agent or the company involved for specialist advice.

Dogs are not allowed to travel loose on aeroplanes but can travel in the hold in a special container. The airline will give you all the details you need about the type of box required, the condition the dog must be in when brought to the airport, and the veterinary certificates you will need. The compartment of the aeroplane in which the dog travels will be specially heated and pressurised so that it will be quite comfortable. However, it is a good idea to get the dog used to its container in advance, if possible. Many international airports have special care centres for animals on long journeys, where they can be let out of their containers for a 'comfort' break.

With the advent of the pets' passport scheme it is possible to travel on holiday to certain countries without the need for quarantine on your return. Details of the scheme can be obtained from the Department of the Environment, Food and Rural Affairs (see page 215).

Dogs, and some other animals, however, need to be boarded in quarantine kennels for six months when they arrive in the UK from some countries. Importation and kennel formalities are usually handled by the transporting company or by a specialist travel agent. If they do not have full facilities for organising this, they will certainly give you all the information you need. Further information can also be obtained from DEFRA.

Chapter 11
Boarding Kennels

There may be times when you will need to leave your dog, because you are going on holiday, for example. When this happens, you will need to find someone to take care of the animal while you are away. You may be fortunate enough to have a friend or member of your family who will take the dog into their home – this is an ideal option, especially if the dog is familiar with the person involved. You should never, however, leave the dog 'home alone', with someone popping in to feed it and let it out for the occasional run. Unlike cats, dogs need company and will become very distressed if left alone like this, even for short periods.

For most people, going away means that the dog will have to be boarded out to kennels. If you have a pedigree dog, your first option is to contact the breeder from whom you bought the dog, as they are sometimes prepared to care for extra animals on request.

If that's not an option, you'll need to find a good local kennels. As with any service, there is a range of options, but the best kennels are run by those who are dog lovers themselves and, believe me, looking after other people's dogs is a great responsibility and one which the best kennel owners take very seriously. Boarding kennels are licensed by local authorities, so you can ask at your local council offices for details of local kennels but it is perhaps better to seek a recommendation from your vet, a local breeder, or another reputable source. Telephone several kennels to see which you like the sound of, then go and have a look at the facilities and accommodation they offer. If they don't allow you to go and visit the kennels, don't leave your dog there.

You should expect your dog to be provided with a clean, dry bed in a kennel of its own, quite separate from other dogs, with its own run area. They will not always be housed indoors but the kennel buildings should be strong enough to stand all weathers. The animals should be provided with plenty to eat and drink, similar to their usual diet, and be taken out for exercise at least twice a day. Some kennels have communal outdoor runs, but I feel a separate walk is better as problems can be passed from one dog to another if they are using the same run. The kennels should obviously be cleaned every day and should be clean and in a good state of repair. The occupants should look happy and well cared for. Every boarding kennels should have comprehensive veterinary insurance – ask to see the certificates if they are not on show.

Find out the costs so you know exactly what you can expect to pay. Most kennels charge on a daily basis, and the charges will increase with the size of the dog. Ask for prices from several kennels so that you can compare them, and remember that the cheapest is not necessarily the best. Check on the opening hours, as some kennels will have specific times for collection and delivery of animals.

The kennel owners, for their part, will want to see evidence of that your dog's vaccinations are up to date, and will not accept the dog unless they have this. Although it is not mandatory in many cases, you may also wish to have your dog inoculated against kennel cough, as this disease is prevalent in many kennels. They may well like to examine your dog on arrival to make sure it is healthy. They may also ask for your holiday address or a telephone number so that they can contact you in case of emergency (although this is very seldom used).

Will my dog pine?

A number of people get worried about the thought of their dog fretting in their absence. In actual fact, this rarely happens, and it is often the case that the dog thoroughly enjoys the change, particularly if it can see other dogs nearby and is in the country where the walks are good.

Having said that, many dogs will go off their food for a day or two, but this is very normal and something kennel owners are used to. They will be keeping a strict eye on whether this is just the dog getting accustomed to the place or whether there is any kind of problem. After all, the food and the surroundings will be slightly different from normal, and the dog will quite naturally wonder where it is. I have often seen a dog reluctant to leave the kennel for a run on the first day, but after a few minutes has been spent gaining the animal's confidence, it trots out quite happily on the lead, and returns with a healthy appetite. By the third day, the dog is behaving as though it has been there for a month!

Dog sitters

Another option is to hire a professional dog sitter, who will look after your dog either in their home or your own while you are away. They have a UK association, NARP, which is a useful source of information (see page 217). They also provide a dog walking service.

Most dog sitters advertise locally, so you make direct contact with them and find out the arrangements and the costs involved, and see whether you get on well with them and would be prepared to trust them with your dog. You'll need to discuss feeding, routines, discipline, and all the aspects of caring for your dog. Always ask for references and always follow them up.

Chapter 12
Showing and Breeding

This is a book about pets rather than showing and breeding, so if you are serious about breeding from your pet, then you need to read more specialist books and discuss it in detail with some experts. However, the following pages should give you a flavour of what is involved.

Showing

If you have a pedigree dog, you might be interested in taking it to local shows. The best way to find out is to ask the breeder or The Kennel Club for information on ringcraft classes and local shows and then go along. You'll be able to find out all the details at first hand, and have a wonderful time seeing the best local shows at the same time.

There are various levels of show, and some people travel vast distances to enter their dogs into the highest-quality shows, so it is a good idea to gain some experience at a more local level before you start to move up the ladder. There are various categories into which you can enter your dog, and you will gradually gain experience in how to present your dog in the best possible way to give it a chance of winning. It is essential to know the standards by which the judges are making their choices by studying The Kennel Club breed standards and the rules of the show. You'll also need to give your dog an extra-special grooming before the event, so find out what is expected and what is not allowed.

Breeding

From my own not inconsiderable personal experience, I can say with assurance that very few people are lucky enough to be able to make dog breeding a profitable living. There are many good reasons for this, any of which you may learn from established breeders. For most breeders, the dogs are their passion, and they use their breeding to supplement another income, rather than replace it. Dog-breeding is a dedicated and time-consuming occupation, demanding a great deal of knowledge and commitment. It involves a great deal more than simply keeping a few bitches of a certain breed and offering the maximum number of puppies to an eagerly expectant market for high prices – as anyone who is serious about the work will already know.

To start with, if you are considering breeding professionally, we can assume that you are fond of dogs, keep at least one, and have become very knowledgeable about that breed. You have probably taken your dog to some shows, and may have won some prizes. The first step, then, is to find out as much as you can about breeding your particular breed. Go to dog shows, talk to local breeders, investigate local breed clubs and contact The Kennel Club.

You need to consider all the following points:

- How will you allocate your time?
- Do you have all the information you need?
- How many breeding bitches do you intend to keep?
- Where the dogs will live?
- What housing and equipment will you need?
- What will it cost to feed, house and care for the dogs?
- What will the veterinary bills be?
- Where will you find the sires?
- How often will you breed?
- How will you match your bitches to the best sires?
- How will the operation be financed?
- What is the market for this breed?
- Are there any health problems associated with the breed?
- Do you have the support of your veterinary surgeon?
- What are the insurance requirements?
- How will you advertise?
- How will you vet prospective purchasers of puppies?

And this is just the start – it is by no means an exhaustive list!

There is also the question of licensing. Anyone breeding more than four litters a year, or who can be shown to be carrying out a business of breeding dogs, requires a licence from their local authority.

Once all this has been resolved, then you will need to find two good breeding bitches. I would not suggest that you rush out to procure a stud dog. Many good ones will be available for reasonable fees, and after you have had one or two good litters you may find among them a dog puppy that may be suitable to be used as a stud by yourself, or hired out to other breeders.

Showing your dogs is an essential part of breeding as it is the best form of advertising, and may result in sales and in contacts with other breeders and exhibitors. It will also keep you up to date with the breed, and possibly result in some awards. However, as I have said, breeding dogs is very much a passion, and the pride in winning a prize or breeding a litter of excellent pups has to be more the motivation than any profit you may – or may not! – make.

Chapter 13
Basic Costs

Obviously the cost of buying and keeping a dog varies tremendously depending on the size and rarity of the dog, your own choice of the type of food and equipment, and so on. This section is intended only to give you some rough guidelines on how much it could cost to keep a dog.

Before embarking on anything that could involve you in substantial expenditure, such as buying your first puppy or sending your dog to a kennels while you are on holiday, it is always best to obtain a few quotations from kennels, breeders or other suitable sources in your area.

Adult dog: An adult dog from a shelter will cost anything up to £100, although some shelters simply ask for a contribution.

Basket or box: From about £10.

Boarding kennels: Prices depend on the size of the dog; a standard poodle costs about £60 per week.

Brush and comb: From about £5.

Collar and lead: From about £8.

Dog coat: From about £15.

Feeding bowl: From about £3.

Food: Good-quality complete dog food costs about £25 for a 15 kg sack. If you decide to feed canned meat, this has to be supplemented with biscuit and works out more expensive overall (£3–£10 weekly, depending on breed, for the meat alone).

Grooming: £15–£35 according to breed. Dogs with coats that require professional grooming should be clipped every 6–12 weeks.

Inoculations: A full course of inoculations for a puppy costs from about £60 but, like vets' fees (see below), this varies greatly. Your pet will require annual boosters and you may also want additional protection against other diseases.

Insurance: From around £200 annually.

Pedigree puppy: An eight-week old puppy of a reasonably common pedigree breed costs anything from £200–£600.

Vet's fees: An initial consultation with your vet will cost on average around £30–£40, but costs vary enormously depending on where you live (it may be cheaper in country areas and you should expect to pay more in Central London) and even from one vet to another, so it is a good idea to shop around. Certainly you should always enquire about costs in advance. If your dog is ill, you will have to pay for every visit to the vet, plus the cost of any medication, so it is well worth insuring your pet.

Further Information

Department of the Environment, Food and Rural Affairs (DEFRA)
Nobel House, 17 Smith Square, London, SW1P 3JR
020 7238 6000
www.defra.gov.uk

British Small Animals Veterinary Association
Woodrow House, 1 Telford Way, Waterwells Business Park,
Quedgeley, Gloucester, GL2 4AB
01452 726700
www.bsava.com

British Veterinary Association
7 Mansfield Street, London, W1G 9NQ
020 7636 6541
www.bva.co.uk

Canine Partners for Independence
Homewell House, 22 Homewell, Havant, Hampshire, PO9 1EE
02392 450156
www.c-p-i.org.uk

Dogs for the Disabled
The Frances Hay Centre, Blacklocks Hill, Banbury, Oxon,
OX17 2BS
01295 252600
www.dogsforthedisabled.org.uk

The Dogs' Home Battersea
4 Battersea Park Road, London, SW8 4AA
020 7622 3626
www.batterseadogshome.com

Guide Dogs for the Blind Association
Burghfield Common, Reading, RG7 3YG
0870 600 2323
www.guidedogs.org.uk

Hearing Dogs for Deaf People
Training Centre, London Road, Lewknor, Oxfordshire,
OX49 5RY
01844 353898
www.hearing-dogs.co.uk

The Kennel Club
1 Clarges Street, London, W1J 8AB
0870 606 6750
www.the-kennel-club.org.uk

National Association of Registered Petsitters
The Pulpits, Little Hereford, Ludlow, SY8 4AY
01584 711534
www.dogsit.com

National Canine Defence League
17 Wakley Street, London, EC1V 7Q
020 7837 0006
www.ncdl.org.uk

People's Dispensary for Sick Animals
Head Office, Whitechapel Way, Priorslee, Telford, TF2 9PQ
01952 290999
www.psda.org.uk

RSPCA
Enquiries Office, Wilberforce Way, Southwater, Horsham,
West Sussex, RH13 7WN
0870 333 5999
24-hour hotline 0870 5555 999
www.rspca.org.uk

Index